GENESIS to REVELATION

PHILIPPIANS, COLOSSIANS
1 AND 2 THESSALONIANS
1 AND 2 TIMOTHY, TITUS
PHILEMON

VAN BOGARD DUNN

PARTICIPANT

GENESIS to REVELATION

PHILIPPIANS, COLOSSIANS
1 AND 2 THESSALONIANS
1 AND 2 TIMOTHY, TITUS
PHILEMON

VAN BOGARD DUNN

PARTICIPANT

GENESIS TO REVELATION SERIES:
PHILIPPIANS, COLOSSIANS, 1 AND 2 THESSALONIANS, 1 AND 2 TIMOTHY, TITUS, PHILEMON
PARTICIPANT

ISBN 9781501855269
3 1969 02568 3060
Manufactured in the United States of America

18 19 20 21 22 23 24 25 26 27—10 9 8 7 6 5 4 3 2 1

ABINGDON PRESS
Nashville

TABLE OF CONTENTS

1

CHRIST'S OBEDIENCE AND CHRISTIAN OBEDIENCE

Philippians 1:1–3:1

DIMENSION ONE: WHAT DOES THE BIBLE SAY?

Answer these questions by reading Philippians 1

1. Who sends the letter to whom? (1:1)

2. How do Paul and Timothy greet the Philippians? (1:2)

3. For what does Paul pray? (1:9)

4. What is Paul's situation as he writes the letter? (1:7, 12-14, 17)

5. How does Paul interpret his situation? (1:12-14)

6. How do Paul's supporters interpret his situation? (1:16)

7. How do his foes interpret it? (1:17)

8. How does Paul expect his situation to turn out? (1:19-26)

9. How does Paul expect the Philippians to act while he is absent? (1:27-30)

Answer these questions by reading Philippians 2:1–3:11

10. What behavior by the Philippians will complete Paul's joy? (2:1-4)

11. What are the marks of this behavior? (2:6-8)

12. Why is this behavior the norm for the Philippians? (2:9-11)

13. What action of Jesus is reproduced in the lives of his followers? (2:12-13)

14. What will make Paul proud "on the day of Christ"? (2:14-18)

15. Whom does Paul plan to send to Philippi soon? Why? (2:19-24)

16. Who came from Philippi to be with Paul and help him? (2:25-30)

17. What do the Philippians hear about Epaphroditus's condition? (2:26-27a, 30)

18. Why does Paul send Epaphroditus back to Philippi? (2:28)

19. What is Paul's basic feeling in this opening section of his letter? (1:4, 18; 2:2, 17-18)

DIMENSION TWO: WHAT DOES THE BIBLE MEAN?

■ **Philippians 1:1-2.** Paul founded the church in Philippi on his second missionary journey (Acts 16:12-40). Although he was forced to flee the city because of persecution (1 Thessalonians 2:2), the church remained loyal to him and, as this letter reveals, was the object of his warm affection. The letter itself expresses Paul's pastoral concern. It follows the usual form of a first-century letter:

    I. Salutation
        A. Sender (1:1a)
        B. Recipient (1:1b)
        C. Greeting (1:20)
    II. Thanksgiving (1:3-11)
    III. Body (1:12-4:20)
    IV. Closing
        A. Greetings (4:21-22)
        B. Benediction (4:23)

Paul uses this conventional pattern to proclaim the gospel to those who could no longer hear his voice, and to assure them of his pastoral care during his absence. Thus, in the salutation of the letter, Paul identifies himself and his colleague Timothy by their primary relationship, servants of Christ Jesus. He also identifies the members of the church at Philippi as "holy people in Christ Jesus" (1:1). Already, then, in these opening verses, Paul affirms that Christ Jesus is the basis of his ministry and the source of the holiness and unity of the church. Paul and Timothy are servants because of the work of Christ in their lives, just as all the members of the church are saints because they are Christ's work.

The gospel that Paul, Timothy, and "all God's holy people" (or saints; 1:1b) have in common is grace, the saving power of God revealed in the Lord Jesus Christ. The lordship of Jesus Christ is not an idea but the power of God that creates servants and saints in the world. The result of grace is peace, the total well-being of the servants and saints of Christ Jesus. The saints (the church at Philippi) enjoy grace and peace, and look forward to receiving them more fully as God's work is perfected in them.

■ **Philippians 1:3-11.** The tension between the *now* and *not yet* of Christian experience comes to voice again in Paul's prayer for the saints. Paul looks back on God's work among the Philippians with thanksgiving for their "partnership in the gospel" (1:5). He looks forward in hope to the completion of their salvation at "the day of Christ Jesus" (1:6). "The day of Christ Jesus" is a technical expression that refers to the coming of Christ in glory at the end of human history to judge and redeem the whole creation. Paul expects Christ to come soon, and his expectation colors all that he writes in this and his other letters. Paul is confident that the grace of God that has brought the Philippians to Christ will also enable them to "be pure and blameless until the day of Christ" (1:10).

■ **Philippians 1:12-14.** Paul's reference to his imprisonment (1:7) is taken up again and interpreted by him as an opportunity to preach the gospel to his captors. He says that such adversity serves to reveal the power of God in which he and other Christians are made confident to speak the word of God boldly and fearlessly.

■ **Philippians 1:15-18.** Paul makes a point of this positive result of his imprisonment because some of his foes have interpreted his imprisonment as evidence of his failure as an evangelist and have used it to discredit his ministry. But regardless of the motivation, the fact that his imprisonment is mentioned by friend and foe alike proclaims Christ and gives Paul reason to rejoice.

■ **Philippians 1:19-26.** Although Paul's imprisonment allows him some freedom to carry on his ministry, his life is, in fact, in jeopardy, and he faces the possibility of martyrdom. Paul looks forward to death as a great benefit for him personally, for it will bring him fully into union with Christ. He also recognizes that God's purpose may require him to continue "in my body" (1:20). Since his life is claimed by God for God's work, Paul is confident that he will be delivered from prison and allowed to return to Philippi to resume his personal ministry there.

■ **Philippians 1:27-30.** Meanwhile, Paul exhorts the Philippians to live a life "worthy of the gospel of Christ" (1:27) whether Paul is present or absent. Such a life is marked by unity of spirit and of mind. Just as Paul's imprisonment is a consequence of his faith, so their faith inevitably involves them in conflict. But that conflict is a sign of their loyalty to Christ and their partnership with Paul in the gospel.

■ **Philippians 2:1-11.** The theme "conduct yourselves in a manner worthy of the gospel" (1:27) is developed more fully in these verses. The exhortations to unity, unselfishness, humility, and a life for others are mandatory for the Philippians because they are revealed in Christ Jesus. Here Paul assumes the pre-existence of Christ as a status that Christ kept, not by grasping for it, but by giving himself in service. His self-giving found full expression in the form of a servant, in a human life of humility and obedience, "even death on a cross" (2:8). Since the crucified Jesus is the revelation of God, he is also the one who has been exalted by God and who will come at the end of human history as the Lord of all history.

The vocation of the Philippians as they await the coming of the Lord in glory is to empty themselves in loving service for one another, even as Jesus Christ emptied himself for them on a cross. Since Christ is a servant for others, they confess their allegiance to him by becoming servants for others.

■ **Philippians 2:12-13.** The keyword for the church as it awaits the completion of God's saving work in human history is *obedience*. The church knows what obedience means because of Jesus' death on a cross. The gospel is not an idea but an act, the act of God in Christ bringing a world that has rebelled against God to acknowledge God in obedient service. The preaching of the gospel, the obedience of Christ Jesus unto death, "even death on a cross," is the power that inspires faith in the world and creates an obedient people, the church. So Paul reminds the Philippians that God brought them to obedience through the gospel, and God continues to call them to obedience, "to will and to act in order to fulfill his good purpose" (2:13).

■ **Philippians 2:14-18.** Paul's mood as he exhorts the church to live "worthy of the gospel of Christ" (1:27) is one of rejoicing because he knows that the victory has already been won. Since God has claimed the whole world in Christ, the Philippians can live for Christ in the world. The victory is not worldly success but the obedience of the cross. Therefore, when the Philippians are partners with Paul in suffering for the gospel, they enter into the victory of the cross that is now hidden in human history but that will be made public "on the day of Christ" (2:16). This faithful participation in the triumph of the gospel is the ground of Paul's rejoicing in his imprisonment and his possible martyrdom.

■ **Philippians 2:19-24.** Paul's confidence in the power of God does not doom him to passive resignation. Rather this confidence releases him to plan and work for the future. He is eager to hear directly from Philippi. So he plans to send Timothy to minister in his place and to bring back firsthand news of the church. Paul is content to do what the situation permits, while still trusting that he will soon be able to visit Philippi himself.

■ **Philippians 2:25–3:1.** Paul has not been out of touch with the Philippians, but rather has heard from them on a number of occasions. They have sent Epaphroditus to cheer him and care for him in prison. But Epaphroditus has been ill, and word of his distress has caused anxiety in Philippi. So Paul sends him back to Philippi to ease their fear and to acknowledge how he represented the church's ministry by caring for Paul.

This whole episode is a dramatic illustration of what it means to live "worthy of the gospel of Christ" (1:27) in a concrete situation. The concern of the church for Paul, the church's distress for Epaphroditus, Paul's anxiety for the church, and Epaphroditus's risking his life for Paul, all witness to the fact that they were all partakers in grace, both in Paul's imprisonment and in "defending and confirming the gospel" (1:7). And since they were partakers in grace in all the circumstances of their fellowship, they were inspired in all the circumstances of their lives to "rejoice in the Lord!" (3:1).

DIMENSION THREE: WHAT DOES THE BIBLE MEAN TO ME?

Philippians 1:1—Who Are We?

Paul's self-understanding and his understanding of the church are summarized in two words: *servants* and *saints* ("holy people" in the NIV). The word that is translated *servants* is better rendered *slaves*. It can be difficult for modern Christians to reflect on what it means to be identified as a *slave* of Christ, because the word itself holds so much negative cultural connotation. It is also so offensive to our usual way of understanding ourselves. We think of ourselves as owned by no one; *slave* reminds us that we are owned by Christ. We think of ourselves as free; *slave* reminds us that we are in bondage to Christ. We think of ourselves as independent; *slave* reminds us that we are dependent on Christ. How does the word *slave* suggest a new way for us to understand ourselves and others? How can we understand Paul's meaning of the word separate from our modern, culturally-imbedded understanding? How does it require us to question the distinctions we make between male and female, clergy and laity, young and old, rich and poor? What other distinctions would be called into question if we identified ourselves as slaves of Christ Jesus?

Paul's other word, *saints*, sounds strange in this context to modern ears. We tend to think of saints as a select group of morally perfect persons. But Paul used the word *saints* to refer to all the members of the church without regard to moral achievement. He could do this because the saints were, for him, the holy ones, those who had been set apart by God's action in Christ for God's service in the world. How does *saints* speak to you about your work in the church and in the world? What specific situations in your church life would have been handled differently if you had remembered that all involved are saints?

Philippians 1:27–2:18—What Must We Do?

Can you recall instances when you were confused about appropriate action because you forgot who you are? Are there other occasions when remembering who you are helped you to will and work for God's good pleasure?

What has God done in Christ for you that transformed your life? Is God still at work in your life? What are some evidences of God's work in your life? How does this give you confidence for the future?

How can we determine whether our lives are worthy of the gospel? What are some of the marks of a manner of life unworthy of the gospel? Can you point to specific actions that seem to be worthy of the gospel? Is suffering a necessary part of a life worthy of the gospel?

Philippians 1:3-11; 2:14-18—What Is Our Hope?

List evidences of the imperfection of the church. Reflect on the condition of the world. How can you engage in this kind of exercise without becoming despondent?

Do you still believe that the name of Jesus is love, the power of God, which will finally bring the whole creation to glorify God in obedient service in "the day of Christ"? If so, what are the implications for our attitude toward persons whom we might dismiss as hopeless? How does this hope speak to us about our personal expectations? What are the points of contact between this hope and efforts to relieve suffering and establish justice throughout the world?

What is the difference between Christian hope and false optimism? How does Christian hope free us from pessimism? How is it possible to rejoice in the midst of conflict and to be glad in suffering?

Our citizenship is in heaven. (3:20)

CHRIST'S RESURRECTION AND CHRISTIAN RESURRECTION

Philippians 3:2–4:23

DIMENSION ONE: WHAT DOES THE BIBLE SAY?

Answer these questions by reading Philippians 3:2-21

1. Paul warns the Philippians to watch out for whom? (3:2)

2. What are Paul's reasons for confidence in the flesh? (3:4-6)

3. What does Paul give up in order to gain Christ? (3:7-9)

4. What are Paul's goals? (3:10-11)

5. What is the one thing Paul does? (3:13-14)

6. Paul tells the Philippians to follow the example of whom? (3:17)

7. What will the Lord Jesus Christ transform when he comes from heaven? (3:20-21)

Answer these questions by reading Philippians 4

8. Whom does Paul mention in 4:2-3?

9. Where are the names of Paul's fellow workers recorded? (4:3)

10. When does Paul tell the Philippians to rejoice? (4:4)

11. What does Paul instruct the Philippians to do to relieve their anxiety? (4:6)

12. How does Paul summarize his words to the Philippians? (4:9)

13. What causes Paul to rejoice greatly in the Lord? (4:10)

14. What is Paul's secret for being well-fed or hungry, living in plenty or in want? (4:12-13)

15. Who helped Paul at the beginning of his ministry? (4:15)

16. What is Paul's motive for accepting help from the Philippians? (4:17)

17. Who will meet all the needs of the Philippians? (4:19)

18. Whom does Paul refer to in his final greeting? (4:22)

DIMENSION TWO: WHAT DOES THE BIBLE MEAN?

■ **Philippians 3:2-11.** Here Paul identifies those who, in his judgment, are a threat to the church: dogs, evil-workers, those who mutilate the flesh. Why does Paul give this passionate warning? Because these persons are corrupting the church by presenting salvation as a human achievement rather than the work of God in Christ. The key phrase is "confidence in the flesh" (3:3), which, in this context, means trust in anything that is not God.

Paul refers to his own experience as a means of reinforcing his argument. His religious heritage as an Israelite, Benjaminite, Hebrew, and Pharisee is renounced as worthless because it separated him from God by encouraging him to strive to earn God's favor. In Christ, Paul has given up his righteousness based on law and has received the righteousness of God founded on faith. *Righteousness* here does not mean right action but rather right relationship. Paul's knowledge of Christ, the crucified and risen Lord, is the basis of his confidence; for in Christ, Paul dies to trusting his own merit and lives to depending on the grace of God. Through faith, Paul enjoys a right relationship to God, not as a status earned, but as a gift freely given.

Paul's life in Christ reproduces the life of Christ, which is described in 2:5-8. The "power of his resurrection" (3:10) is the invincible love of God that is confirmed in human history by sharing in Christ's suffering and "becoming like him in his death" (3:10). So, to the extent that Paul lives the life of love now in service, he participates in the Resurrection now. But, since his mortal body is subject to the power of death, he looks forward to the resurrection from the dead as the completion of his salvation.

■ **Philippians 3:12-16.** Once again Paul expresses the tension between the *now* and *not yet* of Christian experience. The *now* is the love of God in Christ Jesus that has taken hold of Paul and inspires him to strive to live the life of love in the world. The *not yet* is the fact that he is not mature in love and will not be mature in love until the final triumph of love in his life at his resurrection from the dead. Therefore, Paul urges the Philippians in the time between the *now* and *not yet* to hold true to the love of God in the confidence that what God has begun God will complete.

■ **Philippians 3:17-21.** Paul now boldly calls attention to himself as an example to imitate. He can do this because he is nothing in himself but everything in Christ. Christ has made him his own. So as a slave of Christ, Paul dares to tell the Philippians to follow his example rather than the example of those who serve themselves. The contrast is clear and unmistakable. Their end is destruction; his is salvation. Their god is the belly; his is the Creator. They glory in their shame; he glories in the Lord. Their minds are set on earthly things; his on heavenly things. Already Paul lives on earth as if the exalted Lord in heaven had established his reign over the whole creation. Paul no longer trembles in fear of a vengeful judge. Rather, he rejoices in the coming of a Savior, the Lord Jesus Christ, whose final act of love will be to raise him from the dead and give him a body that will no longer be subject to mortality.

■ **Philippians 4:1-7.** To stand firm in the Lord is a possibility for the saints at Philippi because they are no longer in bondage to earthly things but are slaves of Christ, who has set them in his heavenly realm. This is no escape into other-worldliness, but rather an opportunity to witness to the lordship of Christ in their daily relationships. Therefore, Paul tells two quarreling women, Euodia and Syntyche, "be of the same mind in the Lord" (2:7). Their differences involve the whole community, so Paul entreats one of his colleagues at Philippi, a "true companion" (4:3) to help them be reconciled. He also recalls that Euodia and Syntyche, in spite of their differences, are still his partners in the gospel, along with Clement and all his other co-workers, "whose names are in the book of life" (4:3).

Reference to their names being in "the book of life" expresses Paul's confidence that the unity of the church that has been created by the grace of God is stronger than the divisions in the church, and will ultimately prevail. This unwavering hope is voiced once again when he tells them to rejoice. Rejoicing is not to be occasional but continuous, not now and then but always. They can rejoice in all circumstances because all circumstances are opportunities for the saints to witness to their allegiance to the Lord, who is coming soon.

Their witness consists of forbearance, or gentleness, and freedom from anxiety. They can be gentle with one another and with the world because they know that "the Lord is near." They can live without anxiety because God "will guard" (watch over as a sentry; 4:7) their hearts and minds in Christ Jesus. Since their peace is from God, it is absolutely undisturbed by divisions within the church and completely independent of the conditions that prevail in the world.

■ **Philippians 4:8-9.** Paul is rapidly drawing to the close of his letter. As always, he is concerned with the practical affairs of the saints, so he reminds them of the virtues that are recognized in the civilized world and encourages them to think about these virtues. The norm for their behavior, however, is not what is generally accepted in society but rather what they have "learned or received or heard . . . or seen" (4:9) in Paul. Once more, Paul is pointing beyond himself to Christ and declaring his confidence that, when the saints at Philippi join with him in obedience to Christ, they will enter with him into God's peace.

▪ **Philippians 4:10-19.** In this context, Paul receives the gifts the Philippians have sent to him by Epaphroditus. Paul makes it clear that he is sustained in all the circumstances of his life, "whether well fed or hungry, whether living in plenty or in want" (4:12), by God alone. The charity of the saints causes Paul to rejoice because it is a sign of their obedience to Christ in the service of another. Paul refers to the gifts the Philippians sent him in prison as "a fragrant offering, an acceptable sacrifice, pleasing to God" (4:18). Paul rejoices in the gifts because, in the givers, God is glorified.

▪ **Philippians 4:21-23.** Paul closes his letter with the conventional form of farewell greeting. However, once more it is not the form but the substance that distinguishes his relationship with the Philippians. The saints and brothers and sisters who are with Paul at the site of his imprisonment are united with the saints at Philippi by their common participation in Christ Jesus. Therefore, they have a commission that crosses racial and cultural boundaries, and even includes some official representatives of Rome ("Caesar's household," 4:22) in their mutual concern empowered by grace.

DIMENSION THREE: WHAT DOES THE BIBLE MEAN TO ME?

Philippians 3:9—Righteousness

In this verse, Paul contrasts two kinds of righteousness: self-righteousness, based on law, and the righteousness of God, dependent on faith. Self-righteousness assumes that we are capable of earning a place to stand in the presence of God by obeying the rules that God has laid down. The righteousness of God assumes that God's love in Christ gives us a place to stand that we cannot earn but only receive by faith or trust. Paul maintains that a choice must always be made between the two ways of understanding our relationship to God. Are we still confronted with this choice today? Are there signs in our lives that we often are self-righteous? What evidence do we have that sometimes we receive the righteousness of God?

Philippians 3:10-11—Resurrection

Resurrection and righteousness are inseparable in Paul's thought because of his life in Christ. The beginning of Paul's life in Christ is the experience of the resurrected Lord as the gift of God to him while he was still self-righteous, still a sinner, still an enemy of God. Resurrection, for Paul, is the act of God demonstrating that the cross of Jesus Christ is the invincible power of God for the self-righteous, for sinners, for the enemies of God. This act of God connects our lives with the lives of Paul and the saints at Philippi. We know that power of resurrection, not as an idea about immortality or a doctrine of eternal life, but as the forgiveness of our sins that gives us a place to stand in the presence of God. Are resurrection and righteousness inseparable in our experience? How is the experience of forgiveness also an experience of resurrection? Does our relationship to God, our righteousness, always depend on forgiveness? How do we receive forgiveness?

The power of the Resurrection is expressed by sharing in the cross of Jesus Christ. Since the resurrection of Jesus Christ from the dead demonstrates the victory of God's love, we participate in that victory by suffering in the service of others, by carrying a cross, by loving. Resurrection, then, is more than an Easter Sunday celebration. It is also the daily ministry of all the saints who become Christlike in dying to self and living for others. Does ministry always require suffering? In what sense must we die in order to live? Can you think of instances when the church has witnessed to the power of the Resurrection by losing its life? How do we know that love triumphs over death? How does belief in the Resurrection help you continue to grow in your understanding of Christ? What can you say about the resurrection body?

Philippians 4:10-20—Giving

Giving is an essential form of Christian witness because it is the practical expression of the union of the church with its Lord and the union of the saints with one another. Christians do not give in order to achieve a right relationship to Christ or to one another. Instead, they give in response to the relationship that God has already accomplished in Christ and that God will bring to full realization in the resurrection from the dead. Thus, the giving of the saints at Philippi and the giving of the saints in any place, at any time, is the essence of Christian faith and the demonstration of Christian hope. In the final analysis, Christians give because the love of Christ has made them his own and empowered them to give themselves for one another. What is the motive for Christian giving? How is it possible to be in a right relationship to God and ignore the needs of others? What is the relationship between Christ's giving of himself and our giving of ourselves? What makes a gift pleasing and acceptable to God?

So then, just as you received Christ Jesus as Lord, continue to live your lives in him. (2:6)

3

CHRISTIAN FAITH AND CHRISTIAN ACTION

Colossians 1–2

DIMENSION ONE: WHAT DOES THE BIBLE SAY?

Answer these questions by reading Colossians 1

1. Who sends the letter to whom? (1:1-2)

2. What do Paul and Timothy thank God for? (1:3-5)

3. Who is the faithful minister from whom the Colossians learned the gospel? (1:7)

4. What kind of life does Paul pray for the Colossians to lead? (1:10)

5. What do Paul and the Colossians have in Christ? (1:13-14)

6. Who is the head of the church, and who is the body of Christ? (1:18)

7. Through whom does God reconcile all things to himself, and how does God make peace? (1:20)

8. Of what is Paul a servant? (1:23b)

9. In what does Paul rejoice? (1:24)

10. What is the purpose of Paul's servanthood (or ministry)? (1:25)

11. Whom does Paul proclaim? (1:28)

Answer these questions by reading Colossians 2

12. Whom does Paul include with the Colossians in his ministry? (2:1)

13. How is Paul with the Colossians? (2:5)

14. What is "the circumcision not performed by human hands" but "by Christ"? (2:11-12)

15. How does God cancel the legal indebtedness, which stood against us and condemned us"? (2:14)

16. Who is to judge the Colossians "by what you eat or drink, or with regard to a religious festival, a New Moon 0celebration or a Sabbath day"? (2:16)

17. Of what value are "human commands and teachings"? (2:20-23)

DIMENSION TWO: WHAT DOES THE BIBLE MEAN?

■ **Colossians 1:1-2.** Once again, Paul uses the conventional form of a first-century letter to convey his concern for the church at Colossae. But the key words and phrases are distinctly Christian: *apostle, of Christ Jesus, by the will of God, brother, faithful brothers and sisters, in Christ, grace, peace, God our Father.* Although the church is at Colossae, located in a particular place and composed of specific people with a unique history, the reality of the church is defined by relationships that transcend time and place and create a community that is one, holy, and universal. Those relationships are primarily the result of God's action in Christ, the gift of grace that establishes peace.

■ **Colossians 1:3-8.** It seems from this passage that Paul does not have firsthand acquaintance with the church at Colossae. His purpose in this paragraph is to establish common ground with the Colossians by reminding them that "the true message of the gospel that has come" (1:5) to them, is the same message that is preached "throughout the whole world" (1:6). This message, which they have heard from Paul's colleague in ministry, Epaphras, has borne fruit in Colossae in the faith, love, and hope of all the saints. Paul has heard about these fruits of the Spirit from Epaphras and, therefore, gives thanks to God.

■ **Colossians 1:9-14.** Paul's thanksgiving moves smoothly into a prayer of intercession for the Colossians. As we read between the lines, we can surmise that Paul has heard more than good reports from Colossae. Epaphras has also sent him some alarming news about developments there. Apparently, the Colossians are straying away from "the true message" (1:5) to seek a different wisdom and another understanding than they have heard from Epaphras. This seeking has expressed itself in a life unworthy of the Lord and barren of fruit.

All the above is the result of depending on a power other than the power of God's love revealed in God's beloved Son. It is nothing less than a rejection of the rule of Christ, "the inheritance of his holy people in the kingdom of light," to return to "the dominion of darkness" (1:12-13). What Paul declares in his prayer of petition is that, in the forgiveness of sins, the Colossians have already experienced in Christ the full revelation of God that will enable them to endure with patience, joy, and thanksgiving. To be enticed away from this truth is to reject the light for the darkness and to forfeit one's place in the kingdom of Christ.

■ **Colossians 1:15-20.** The false teaching that Paul alludes to in his passage of intercession is a threat to the Colossians because it arises from an inadequate understanding of Christ. So Paul goes on the attack by using the language of those who claim to have a superior knowledge of God, given in another revelation, to declare that Christ's revelation is the full and final revelation of God's nature and work. Everything that the false teachers claim to find in another revealer is not only unnecessary but wrong because it is a denial of the reconciling work of God in the cross of Christ.

Christ is superior to all other rivals for four reasons: (1) "he is the image of the invisible God" (1:15); (2) he is the agent of God in creation; (3) he is the head of the church; and (4) he is the agent of God in reconciliation. What Paul declares about Christ as revealer, creator, and head of the church is the result of what he has experienced in Christ as the agent of God's love, forgiving him of his sins and enabling him to live in peace. Paul experienced God's "fullness" in the crucified and risen Lord. Therefore, the cross becomes, for Paul, the revelation of God's creative and redemptive purpose for all creation.

■ **Colossians 1:21-23.** The reconciling work of Christ is the common experience that binds Paul and the Colossians together. What he affirms in 1:15-20 is what they have experienced through the ministry of Epaphras. The practical consequence of this experience is that, when they remember who they are—saints made holy, blameless, and irreproachable by the self-giving love of God in Christ—they will act like saints. What the Colossians need is not some new doctrine or teaching but stability and steadfastness in the faith, in the gospel that they have heard and of which Paul is a servant.

■ **Colossians 1:24–2:5.** The gospel for Paul is the self-giving love of God in Christ. Response to the gospel is participation in that self-giving love. Paul's apostolic work as a minister, or servant, of the church is accompanied by suffering, but is the occasion for joy; for, in it, the saving work of Christ is continued and made available to the church. Also, Paul's ministry to the Gentiles makes known the mystery of God's saving purpose, the all-inclusive love of God in Christ. This love is the content of Paul's preaching and the power that inspires him to serve. The mystery is not given to a select group of initiates into a secret order; it is preached publicly to all so that all may receive wisdom and the love of God, and all may become mature instruments of love.

Paul calls attention to his apostolic ministry because, in his service, the universal gospel of Christ is at work. Therefore, he breaks his usual custom of limiting his ministry to churches he has founded, and includes those who have not seen his face at Colossae and Laodicea. He does this because, in his judgment, they are being led by false teachers to depend on something other than the love of God in Christ. Paul reaches out to them in love, in the confidence that his love will remind them of their faith in Christ. What they lack is not the beguiling and deluding promises of more understanding and knowledge but the assurance that they are loved by God and empowered by love to share in God's work.

■ **Colossians 2:6-23.** This entire section contains Paul's warning against false teaching. He opens the section by reminding the Colossians that the authentic teaching is the tradition about Christ they have received from faithful ministers such as Epaphras. This teaching also contains instruction about the way Christians should live. The content of the faith is Christ Jesus the Lord, and the practical expression of the faith is the life that Christ enables his followers to live, the life of self-giving love. The lordship of Christ is not a burden to be endured but a gift to be received in thanksgiving.

This summary of true teaching and its expression in faithful living is followed in 2:8-15 by a stern warning against false doctrine. The central concern is to affirm the absolute finality and complete sufficiency of the cross. In the cross, God has triumphed over all the enemies of human life and established in human history the reign of Christ. Nothing more needs to be done, and nothing more needs to be known.

The church is the community where the rule of Christ is acknowledged and enjoyed. One enters the rule of Christ not by works but by grace, which is symbolized by baptism. Baptism is a dramatic portrayal of the work of God whereby the individual dies to dependence on the flesh and lives to dependence on God. The gospel of the crucified and risen Lord that is proclaimed in words is also acted out in the ritual of baptism. The action represented in baptism enables the church to receive the love of Christ and to live out that love in faithful service. Just as the gospel is not an idea but the action of Christ, so the life of faith is not an idea but the work of Christ. According to Paul, any addition or subtraction from this teaching is an empty deceit.

Paul moves quickly from a warning about false doctrine to a warning about false practice. Again the central concern is the lordship of Christ in the church and in the world. No principalities or powers remain that need to be appeased by dietary laws or ritual observances because they have all been overcome by Christ. Christ has revealed God's "fullness" (2:9). Therefore, all other visions and messengers (angels) have no authority. Only Christ is the legitimate head of the church because, in him, all the parts are united and nourished by the love of God.

Again Paul reminds the Colossians of their baptism as a mark of the gospel action by which they are dead to the world and alive to Christ. Since that is the case, they no longer need to depend on the world or the flesh for their salvation. They are acceptable to God, not because they earn God's favor by religious ritual or ascetic discipline, but because in Jesus' cross they are forgiven of their sins; and in his resurrection they are empowered to live as his servants in the world. Therefore, false practice, whether liturgical or moral, is worthless because it is self-righteousness, "sensual indulgence" (2:23).

DIMENSION THREE: WHAT DOES THE BIBLE MEAN TO ME?

Colossians 1:7-8; 1:24–2:5—The Authority of Right Leaders

What understanding of leadership prevails in the church today? Which attitudes would have to be changed if Paul's understandings were to become normative?

Paul and Epaphras were ministers of the gospel, and as such they were responsible for preaching and teaching. This role of leadership is still current but often obscured by other responsibilities such as administration and pastoral care. Leaders may become preoccupied with other concerns and neglect the ministry of the word as it is explained in Colossians. Is this true because the church has become a complex institution? How may this development be accommodated without losing sight of the central importance of preaching and teaching for the life of the church?

Colossians 1:15-20—The Content of True Teaching

I know of no simple or easy solution to the problem created by rival claims to the truth made by sincere and honest persons. Perhaps Colossians helps us deal with the problem, not by giving us a final answer, but by helping us live faithfully with our differences. Do you agree with Paul that the content of Christian truth is defined by Christ's death and resurrection? Is it possible to have different understandings of what Christ's death and resurrection mean and still be one body in Christ? Why or why not?

Colossians 2:16-23—The Source of Right Action

Faithful Christians can express their obedience to Christ in different forms of ethical and liturgical action. For example, one group of Christians may confess the lordship of Christ by abstaining from alcoholic beverages. Another group may confess his lordship by the temperate use of alcoholic beverages. In light of the argument developed in Paul's letter to the Colossians, what might be wrong about either abstinence or temperance would be claiming that one was saved by abstinence or temperance instead of by the grace of God in Christ. What is absolutely intolerable is the confession of any power as lord except Jesus Christ, crucified and raised from the dead. What liturgical and ethical actions are prohibited by Paul's argument in Colossians? How does his argument help you decide about these matters today? Does it help you to be more tolerant of others?

Whatever you do, whether in word or deed, do it all in the name of the Lord Jesus, giving thanks to God the Father through him. (3:17)

RELATIONSHIPS IN THE NEW LIFE

Colossians 3–4

DIMENSION ONE: WHAT DOES THE BIBLE SAY?

Answer these questions by reading Colossians 3

1. What does Paul tell the Colossians to set their hearts on? (3:1)

2. Where is Christ? (3:1)

3. Where is the life of the Colossians hidden? (3:3)

4. What have the Colossians taken off, and what have they put on? (3:9-10)

5. Who is all and in all? (3:11)

6. How must the Colossians forgive one another? (3:13)

7. What does Paul want to rule in their hearts? (3:15)

8. Whom does Paul speak to in 3:18-22 and 4:1?

9. Whom do the Colossians work for, and who will reward them? (3:23-24a)

Answer these questions by reading Colossians 4

10. What does Paul ask that they pray for? (4:2-3)

11. Where is Paul? Why is he there? (4:3)

12. How are the Colossians to act toward outsiders? (4:5)

13. Whom does Paul send to the Colossians? (4:7, 9)

14. Who is with Paul in prison? (4:10)

15. Who joins Aristarchus in sending greetings to the Colossians? (4:10-14)

16. To whom does Paul ask the Colossians to send greetings at Laodicea? (4:15)

17. What word does Paul send to Archippus? (4:17)

18. Who writes the closing greeting? (4:18)

DIMENSION TWO: WHAT DOES THE BIBLE MEAN?

■ **Colossians 3:14.** Paul now instructs the Colossians about how they should behave in the new life. Everything depends on what God has done in Christ. Once again, Paul uses the imagery of the ritual of baptism to announce that the Christian has been raised with Christ to live under the reign of Christ. The Christian's earthly existence is now the sphere of Christ's rule, for the Christian has died to self and lives to God. By faith, the Christian enjoys now the resurrection life as it is hidden in human history under the sign of the cross. Resurrection will not be fully experienced by the Christian, however, until the coming of Christ at the end, when what is now hidden with Christ in suffering will be manifest with him in glory.

Paul argues in these verses that, since the Christian has been given a new center of life in the love of Christ, everything that the Christian does is now controlled by that center. In the following verses Paul develops what this means negatively (3:5-11) and positively (3:12-17) for the Christian life.

■ **Colossians 3:5-11.** First, making Christ's love the center of life means the death of self as the center of life. "Whatever belongs to your earthly nature" (3:5) does not refer to the so-called desires of the flesh, but to any thought or action that claims for self what belongs only to God. Paul lists five expressions of the self-centered life: sexual immorality, impurity, lust, evil desires, and greed. The first four are sexual sins. They are probably to be understood here as arising from the fifth, greed or covetousness, which Paul often presents as the basic form of sin from which all other sins spring. Notice, what he condemns is not sex as such but sex as self-indulgence. When self claims everything for self alone (greed), then all other relationships are ruined. All these actions are forms of idolatry because they claim absolute worth for a part of creation instead of ascribing absolute worth to the Creator.

Since the Christian is given a new center of life in Christ, everything that arises from a self-centered life must be renounced or put away. Again, Paul has a list of five: anger, rage, malice, slander, and filthy language. Maybe he is reminding the Colossians that the words that give expression to the self also reveal the self's allegiance. If the center is false, then the expression will be false. If the center is true, then the truth will control talk from the mouth.

Paul uses language that seems to come directly from the baptismal liturgy: "[take] off your old self' and "put on the new self" (3:9-10). Perhaps he has in mind the symbolism of taking off the old garments in preparation for baptism and receiving the new garments after the ritual. What is certain is that Paul understands the old nature in terms of the rebellion of the creation against the Creator and the new nature in terms of the obedience of the creation to the Creator. The old life of disobedience, which destroyed the image of God in creation, has been restored by the obedience of Christ, so that those who die and rise with Christ are restored to the image of God. The image of the Creator, then, is the self-giving love of God as shown in the life, death, and resurrection of Jesus. This image is shared by all who have faith in the Lord Jesus Christ.

The practical result is that all the old distinctions—Greek and Jew, circumcised and uncircumcised, barbarian, Scythian, slave, free person—no longer apply. Christ is the universal reality that establishes the worth of all persons. In Christ, all persons are related to one another in love.

■ **Colossians 3:12-17.** The second meaning of "set your minds on things above" (3:2) is that God's choice of the saints enables them to live as the "chosen people, holy and dearly loved." Paul tells them to put on a manner of life that expresses the fact that they no longer live for self but for others. The qualities of such a life are compassion, kindness, humility, gentleness, and patience. Although this list of five virtues could be found in the common ethical teaching of the first-century world, Paul is not advocating the conventional morality of the day. He is reminding the Colossians that Christ is at work in them producing works that are pleasing to God. Since Christ has put all sinners first by forgiving their sins, they must forgive one another.

The finality of Christ as revealer and redeemer is his love for all. His love is the power that unites the church and all creation in a harmonious whole. To "put on love" (3:14) is to put on Christ and to settle all matters of thought and action by submitting them to Christ. The result is peace, the total well-being of a body in which all the parts work for the good of the whole. Since peace is always a gift of pure grace, those who receive it are thankful.

Paul's confidence arises, not from optimism about human potential, but from trust in "the word of Christ" to control the lives of those who have received it in faith. When hard decisions about doctrine and behavior confront the Colossians, it is the "message of Christ" (3:16) that guides them. Also in their public worship, they are inspired by "the message of Christ" to respond to God as they "sing psalms, hymns and songs from the Spirit . . . with gratitude" (3:16).

Thus, the challenge of the false teachers is met in the church by the indwelling power of Christ, which unites the church in liturgical and ethical behavior well-pleasing to God. The church is accountable only to God because it is the creation of God in Christ. All that it does is "in the name" or in the power of the Lord Jesus. Thanksgiving is not a formal expression of gratitude but the entire life of the congregation, united in faithful service to God by the self-giving love of Christ.

■ **Colossians 3:18–4:1.** Here Paul develops what it means to "put on the new self" in terms of concrete relationships. Just as Christ's love has set the Colossians in a radically new relationship to God, so it has set them in radically new relationships to one another. The new nature, life for others, is not an abstraction but the specific obligation of wives, husbands, children, fathers, slaves, and masters to honor Christ within the social structures of first-century life.

Paul does not start a revolution to change the social organization of the ancient world. Instead, he announces a radically new orientation of life that brings all social structures under the judgment of God and transforms them into opportunities for faithful service. All are now slaves of Christ; whatever their status in life—wife, husband, child, father, slave, master—they all are under the same mandate: "Whatever you do, whether in word or deed, do it all in the name of the Lord Jesus, giving thanks to God the Father through him" (3:17).

■ **Colossians 4:2-4.** Everything at Colossae depends on how the saints live out of their relationship to God. So Paul, as he draws to the close of his letter, reminds them to maintain that relationship in steadfast and watchful prayer. Paul recognizes that his life also depends solely on God. So the only thing that he asks of the Colossians is that they pray for him. Paul does not request prayer for privilege but for service: opportunity to preach the gospel plainly, although it has already made him a prisoner.

■ **Colossians 4:5-6.** Paul is concerned not only with the internal relationships of the saints but also their conduct toward the world. The most powerful evangelizing force available to the church is the witness that the church is called to make as God's people who live in the world but are not of the world. To act wisely is to act out of love in an unloving society. To speak graciously, or "seasoned with salt" (4:6), is nothing more than to express faith in Christ in all one's conversation with an unfaithful world.

■ **Colossians 4:7-17.** The closing personal greetings of the letter show how Paul lives out what it means for him to "put on the new self." He does this in the context of a network of personal relationships that bind him to the Colossians although they have not seen his face. His experience of the body of Christ is the concrete reality of communion with real people.

Paul seems to have a particular purpose in mind as he mentions these persons. In the case of Tychicus and Onesimus, he sends them to Colossae so that the Colossians will have a firsthand report of how Paul is doing in prison. Aristarchus, Mark, and Justus are singled out to remind the Gentile Christians that Paul is also in close relationship to Jewish Christians. He calls attention to Epaphras to show, once again, the solidarity of faithful preachers of the gospel. He mentions Luke and Demas by name to help the Colossians appreciate the fact that Paul takes part in a community that includes those present with him in prison and those with whom he is present in spirit. He sends greetings to Nympha and the church in her house as a way of reminding them that the ties of Christian love that bind Paul to the Colossians also bind the Colossians to the Laodiceans. Finally, he names Archippus to emphasize that ministry is always a call to service directed to a specific individual in a particular place.

All these references tell of Paul's love for the Colossians, for those present with him in prison, and for the Laodiceans. They also express their love for him and for one another. Since all have "put on the new self," they cannot have any distinctions among them (3:10-11). Paul certifies this, not merely by concluding the letter in his own hand, but by living the content of the letter as a faithful minister of the gospel.

DIMENSION THREE: WHAT DOES THE BIBLE MEAN TO ME?

Colossians 3:1-11—The Image of God

We often think of *image* as physical likeness. *Image* in this context does not refer to physical likeness but to representing God and doing God's work. How do we know what it means to represent God on earth? What is God's work that we are called to do?

Can you think of ways that the image of God is distorted by our actions? Are these distortions of God's image related to disobeying God? If so, how?

Colossians 3:12-13—Forgiving One Another

The Christian life, as Paul interprets it in Colossians, is primarily relational. The basis of all Christian relationships is what God does for the world in Christ. A good summary of this is given in 1:13-14. Do you feel that you have been delivered from darkness? What does it mean to be brought into the kingdom of Christ? Do we receive redemption when our sins are forgiven? Explain your answer.

Does the ritual of baptism help you experience anew the compassion, kindness, humility, gentleness, and patience of Christ? Are these qualities reproduced in the community created by Christ? How can we enjoy these qualities personally but refuse to live them in relation to one another? How does baptism help us forgive one another?

Colossians 3:18–4:1—Social Responsibility

How do Paul's words to the Colossians about household duties apply today? Paul summarizes his position in 3:17. Does this word apply to us when we must make difficult decisions in family, government, education, commerce, and industry? Must the Christian be content to work within structures as they are; or is the Christian called to work to change structures? How can change be accomplished?

For what is our hope, our joy, or the crown in which we will glory in the presence of our Lord Jesus when he comes? Is it not you? Indeed, you are our glory and joy. (2:19-20)

5
COMFORT IN DISTRESS

1 Thessalonians 1–3

DIMENSION ONE: WHAT DOES THE BIBLE SAY?

Answer these questions by reading 1 Thessalonians 1

1. Who sends the letter to whom? (1:1)

2. What does Paul remember about the Thessalonians? (1:3)

3. How did the gospel come to the Thessalonians? (1:5)

4. To whom do the Thessalonians become a model? (1:7)

Answer these questions by reading 1 Thessalonians 2

5. Where had Paul and his associates suffered and been insulted? (2:2)

6. Whom do Paul and his co-workers speak to please? (2:4)

7. Why do Paul and those who serve with him as evangelists work day and night? (2:9)

8. What does Paul encourage, comfort, and urge the Thessalonians to do? (2:11-12)

9. Who has stopped Paul from coming to the Thessalonians? (2:18)

10. What is Paul's "hope . . . joy, or the crown in which we will glory" before the Lord Jesus at his coming? (2:19-20)

Answer these questions by reading 1 Thessalonians 3

11. Whom does Paul send from Athens to minister to their needs? (3:1-2)

12. What encourages Paul in his distress and persecution? (3:7)

13. Who may clear Paul's way to the Thessalonians? (3:11)

14. Who establishes the Thessalonians blameless and holy in the presence of God? When? (3:12-13)

DIMENSION TWO: WHAT DOES THE BIBLE MEAN?

■ **1 Thessalonians 1:1.** Paul begins with the characteristic salutation and greeting of a first-century letter. These conventions are Christianized by the fact that Paul, Silas, and Timothy are bound to the Thessalonians by the action of God in the Lord Jesus Christ. That action is summarized by the word *grace*, the self-giving love of God. The result of that action is *peace*, the total well-being of a community reconciled to God and to one another by God's saving work in Christ.

■ **1 Thessalonians 1:2-10.** Just as Paul uses the conventional form of salutation and greeting in 1:1 to express the reality of the one, holy, universal church; so in this section, the usual expression of thanksgiving becomes an unusual proclamation of the gospel that has created the Gentile churches. Through these verses we are privileged to hear the gospel as it was preached by Paul. Although we cannot be absolutely certain, Paul is probably writing from Athens about AD 51, to continue by letter the ministry he had begun in person and longs to resume in person as soon as possible. During this absence, the most important thing he can do for the Thessalonians is to remind them of what brought him to them in the first place, how he carried out his ministry, and the response created in them by his ministry.

Paul's ministry to the Thessalonians was not Paul's idea, but rather the working out in human history of God's saving purpose. Of course Paul is the agent, but the power comes from God. So when Paul reminds the Thessalonians of their beginning in the gospel, the emphasis falls primarily on God, the Lord Jesus Christ, and the Holy Spirit; and only secondarily on Paul, his associates, and the converts at Thessalonica. In this section, for example, God is mentioned by name six times; Christ or the Lord or Jesus or the Son, five times; and the Holy Spirit, twice. According to Paul's understanding, when he came to Thessalonica, he found

God, the Lord Jesus Christ, and the Holy Spirit already at work. Paul's preaching was simply the announcement of what God had done, was doing, and would do in the Lord Jesus Christ. Paul did not convince the Thessalonians that the gospel was true. Rather the Holy Spirit convicted them of the truth of the message. Their response (1:3) was a sign that they had been chosen by God to take part in God's saving work in the world.

The work of the Holy Spirit enabled the Thessalonians to imitate Paul and the Lord. The point that the apostle makes here is that the Spirit equips the saints for faithful ministry as they hear and obey the gospel. Just as Jesus' obedience and Paul's apostleship involved them in conflict and suffering, so the Thessalonians discover that their faith exposes them to the affliction of a hostile world. Their suffering, instead of filling them with sorrow, is the occasion for rejoicing; for it is a sign that they are God's agents of salvation in the world. Their Spirit-empowered ministry spreads the gospel message everywhere, so that they are, themselves, the fruit of Paul's labor.

The church is not neutral territory. The church is the community of those who have turned from idol worship to worship of God revealed in the Lord Jesus Christ. This worship is the public acknowledgment that the crucified and risen Lord is the ultimate power of the universe. The form of this public acknowledgment is twofold. In the first place, it is a life of service now in response to the life and truth revealed in the Lord Jesus Christ. In the second place, it is a life of confident hope that what God has begun in the resurrection of Jesus Christ, God will complete when Christ comes from heaven to judge and redeem the whole creation. The two words Paul uses here to summarize the life of the church, *serve* and *wait*, remind the Thessalonians that response to the gospel always takes place in the time of tension between the *now* and *not yet* of salvation.

■ **1 Thessalonians 2:1-12.** Now Paul turns to a review of his ministry among the Thessalonians. He does this, not to defend himself, but to show how the gospel gives meaning and purpose to his life. His primary purpose in this entire section is to remind the Thessalonians that his life among them was in every respect the result of God's action in the Lord Jesus Christ. Paul's ministry has been fruitful because God has given him courage to proclaim the gospel of God "in the face of strong opposition" (2:12). Faithfulness to the message is the standard against which he judges his ministry. Therefore, Paul is freed from striving to win the approval of human beings by knowing that he is accountable only to God, who is the sole judge of his work.

Paul's faithfulness to his divinely appointed task has enabled him to have the right relationship to the Thessalonians. Since he is preoccupied with doing God's work, he is no longer concerned about his status or about the impression he makes on others. In the service of the gospel of God, he is freed from self-service so that he can live for others. Paul is not concerned about his welfare but committed to giving himself in gentle, affectionate care for the well-being of those who have become dear to him.

Paul also reminds the Thessalonians that his ministry was confirmed among them by his giving up all claims of human glory in order to fulfill his calling. Specifically, he worked to support himself, so that his preaching the gospel was no burden to the Thessalonians. Paul's authority is defined in this context as the self-giving love of ministry that expresses itself in pastoral care. All this is controlled by a practical concern: that as the Thessalonians are reminded of Paul's behavior when he was with them, they will be motivated to imitate him now in his absence. The center of attention in Paul's encouraging, comforting, and urging is not Paul but God, who calls the Thessalonians "into his kingdom and glory" (2:12). Just as the apostolic call made Paul a man for others, the call of the Thessalonians makes them a community for others. Their only concern is "to live lives worthy of God" (2:12).

■ **1 Thessalonians 2:13–3:13.** The sequence of Paul's thought unfolds quite logically: 1:2-10, a summary of the apostolic message; 2:1-12, a reminder of the apostolic ministry; and 2:13–3:13, a call to faithfulness in affliction. The connecting link that binds these three parts together in a unified argument is the gospel that Paul brought to the Thessalonians. The gospel continues to be the basis of Paul's ministry to them while he is separated from them. The Thessalonians hear "the word of God" (2:13) not as an idea, but as the powerful presence of God's love bringing them from unfaith to faith, from the worship of idols to the service of the true and living God. "The word of God," the gospel, continues its work among the Thessalonians and is the basis for all that Paul now has to say about their relationship to the world, to Paul, and to one another. "The word of God" is an absolute claim on those who hear. For them, there is no middle ground, only an opportunity for decision.

The believers in Thessalonica are joined to the churches in Judea by the fact that their obedience to God arouses the same hostility that Jesus and the prophets experienced because of their loyalty to God. The distinctive mark of faith, wherever it occurs—among the Gentiles or in Judea—is suffering at the hands of the unfaithful enemies of God. The final destiny of all who refuse to obey God is inevitable. Upon them the wrath of God has already come in the sense that they are separated from the source and goal of their existence by rebellion against God.

By contrast, Paul's obedience to God's saving purpose as an apostolic minister unites him with all the saints at Thessalonica. This union with them does not depend on physical presence, for even in his enforced absence, they are present in his heart and the object of his eager endeavor and great desire. This feeling is more than the warm affection of a friend for his dear companions. It is also the supreme confidence of a faithful minister in the power of God's love to overcome all obstacles and create a community that even Satan is powerless to destroy. So Paul is reassured (in circumstances that appear to contradict all that he has worked to achieve) by the recollection that the same love

45

that called the Thessalonians to faith will enable them to stand firm until the coming of the Lord Jesus. Just as Paul and the saints share in the suffering of Christ, so they will share in the glory and joy of the victory of Christ over sin and death. This assurance is Paul's hope and joy and glory.

All this, however, is not a flight from the pain of separation or escape from anxiety about the welfare of loved ones. On the contrary, it moves Paul to give up the company of Timothy so that he may come to them to minister in the apostle's place. Timothy's message is a clear call to stand firm in affliction by remembering that suffering is the destiny of all who hear the word of God. What motivates Paul is once again his passionate concern for the welfare of the Thessalonians.

Timothy returns to Paul with good news that the love that binds the apostle to his converts also binds them to him. This news of the triumph of the gospel, the word of God, in Thessalonica comforts Paul in his distress and affliction. The victory inspires him to bring this section of his letter to a close as he began it, with thanksgiving to God. Although Paul is reassured by Timothy's report, he is by no means complacent. He continues to pray that God's love will find concrete expression in his life by making it possible for him to visit Thessalonica again. Paul also prays that the Thessalonians will increase and abound in love, not only to one another, but to all; so that God's work of love begun in Christ will be completed by Christ's coming as the judge and redeemer of all creation.

DIMENSION THREE: WHAT DOES THE BIBLE MEAN TO ME?

1 Thessalonians 1:6-7; 2:14-17; 3:1-7—
The Affliction of the Church

Our situation is radically different from the Thessalonian situation. Can you identify the differences? Do these differences help explain why preaching and hearing the word today are hardly ever the occasion for conflict and suffering? Granted that our situation is different from the Thessalonian situation, does that mean that the word of God is different? Which specific characteristics of the word of God are always the same? How does the Bible help you identify these characteristics? Paul does not use "the word of God" (2:13) in this context to refer to the Bible but to the preaching of the gospel. Can you recall times when the preaching of the gospel created conflict and suffering for the church? Have you experienced any affliction that has been caused by your allegiance to Christ?

The church feels great pressure to conform to the standards and expectations of society. Do you feel this pressure? What evidence is there that these pressures were already being felt by the Thessalonians? What guidance does Paul give the Thessalonians to help them withstand the temptation to conform to society? What relevance does this have for the contemporary church?

1 Thessalonians 3:6-8—The Comfort of the Church

Why are we tempted to become self-centered in times of distress and affliction? Why do we find comfort by escaping from distress and affliction? Recall times of comfort that came to you in distress and affliction as a result of caring for another person and receiving care yourself.

One important distinction to make in this regard is the difference between a comfortable church and a church that is comforting. What questions does this raise about the preoccupation with comfort in the modern church? Has comfort become our idol? How does God's call addressed to us through Paul challenge us to turn away from our comfortable ease to become agents of comfort in a world of distress and affliction?

May God himself, the God of peace, sanctify you through and through. May your whole spirit, soul and body be kept blameless at the coming of our Lord Jesus Christ. (5:23)

6

THE COMING OF THE LORD

1 Thessalonians 4–5

DIMENSION ONE: WHAT DOES THE BIBLE SAY?

Answer these questions by reading 1 Thessalonians 4

1. What have the Thessalonians learned from Paul? (4:1)

2. Who gives the Holy Spirit to the Thessalonians? (4:8)

3. Whom does God teach them to love? (4:9)

4. On whom are they to be dependent? (4:12)

5. What does Paul believe about Jesus? (4:14)

6. How will the Lord come from heaven? (4:16)

7. Who will rise first? (4:16)

8. What will happen to those who are alive when the Lord comes from heaven? (4:17)

Answer these questions by reading 1 Thessalonians 5

9. How will "the day of the Lord" come? (5:2)

10. Why won't the day of the Lord surprise the faithful? (5:4)

11. What are the Thessalonians to do in preparation for the day of the Lord? (5:6)

12. What are they to put on? (5:8)

13. What are the Thessalonians to do for one another? (5:11)

14. Whom does Paul beseech them to respect, hold in highest regard, and love? (5:12-13)

15. With whom does Paul urge them to be patient? (5:14)

16. When are the Thessalonians to give thanks? (5:18)

17. How are they to greet "all God's people"? (5:26)

DIMENSION TWO:
WHAT DOES THE BIBLE MEAN?

■ **1 Thessalonians 4:1-8.** In the first three chapters of this letter, Paul proclaims the basic message that creates and sustains the church. He turns in these last two chapters to exhort, advise, and edify the Thessalonians about matters of sexual morality, relationships within the community, the fate of those who have died before the coming of the Lord, the manner of the Lord's coming, preparation for his coming, and church order and discipline. Paul needs to deal with the details of daily conduct because the crucified and risen Lord claims all life as the realm of redemption. Therefore, his lordship must be expressed by obedient service in every aspect of human existence.

In this particular section, Paul reminds the Thessalonians of how they ought to live and to please God. This direction is more than a vague generality; it is a specific claim that requires a concrete response. Paul's concern here is not just his opinion, since he gives this instruction by the authority of the Lord Jesus and according to the will of God. What is at issue is God's work in Christ that has as its goal the sanctification or holiness of God's people. Because they belong to God in Christ, they can no longer live for themselves in any human relationship. Therefore, they are called from all forms of sexual indulgence and told to fulfill their marital duties as God's obedient servants.

■ **1 Thessalonians 4:9-12.** Since the claim of God on human life is absolute, the response of God's people is always imperfect and open to constant growth and reformation. This is especially true as the church reviews its internal relationships. God teaches the church to love, not by words alone, but by God's self-giving love in Jesus Christ. The reality of the church is established in God's love, but in actuality the church is always becoming what it is in God's purpose. Therefore, Paul's direction to love "more and more" is always in order. The direction to love more and more is not a vague generality but a specific command: "make it your ambition to lead a quiet life: You should mind your own business and work with your hands" (4:11). Paul commends these disciplines of love so that the gospel will be proclaimed in the life of the community, and the community will be free to carry out its evangelistic work in the world.

■ **1 Thessalonians 4:13-18.** Paul's experience of the saving work of God in Christ Jesus claimed him so completely that he lived as if that work had already been consummated. This central experience of his life expressed itself in his tireless labor as an apostle and in his confident hope that Christ would come soon to complete God's saving purpose for all creation. The coming of the Lord was an integral part of his preaching and had been received well by the Thessalonians. But since Paul's departure from Thessalonica, some of the believers have died. Their surviving loved ones are concerned about what would happen to them because they had died before the coming of the Lord. They asked Paul about this issue, and he responds in these verses.

Paul writes as a pastor to grieving parishioners and brings the full resources of the gospel to bear on the problem. The gospel is what God has done in the death and resurrection of Jesus Christ. Since God's love has been fully revealed in the cross and fully vindicated in the Resurrection, nothing can separate believers from that love, not even death. So the fact that some have died before the coming of the Lord is of no consequence. They are safe in the keeping of God, who will provide for them a place of honor in the final act of salvation, regardless of when it happens. Paul sends this message to the grieving Thessalonians. The only thing that really matters is their faith that the Lord will come to complete what God has begun: the sanctification of God's people and the salvation of the world.

Paul uses the traditional language of first-century Jewish literature to affirm his faith: "The Lord himself will come down from heaven, with a loud command, with the voice of the archangel and with the trumpet call of God" (4:16). The meaning of these conventional symbols is clarified and enlarged by taking part in the confidence of the gospel: "We will be with the Lord forever" (4:17). This belief is the basis of Christian hope whether one is asleep or alive in the Lord, and it is the ultimate reassurance for those who grieve. "Therefore encourage one another with these words" (4:18).

■ **1 Thessalonians 5:1-11.** Since the coming of the Lord had been delayed, some Thessalonians were concerned about when it would occur. Paul's response is clear and unequivocal: *When* is not the issue, for no one knows. The real issue is that the coming of the Lord will come as a surprise, with no warning, "like a thief in the night" (5:2). But in Christ the new age of light has invaded the old age of darkness so that the coming of the light in full splendor at the end will not surprise those who already, by faith, belong to the day and to the light. One prepares for the coming of the Lord by living now as if the end has already come, by turning away from the false peace and security of the age of darkness, and by living in the light.

The invasion of the new age of light into the old age of darkness is the occasion for taking part now in the final victory of light over darkness. So the time of waiting for the coming of the Lord is a time of warfare, a time to be awake and sober. But light does not triumph over darkness by taking the weapons of darkness. Rather, light triumphs by being faithful to the light. Therefore, Paul urges the Thessalonians to put on the armor of light: "putting on faith and love as a breastplate, and the hope of salvation as a helmet" (5:8).

Paul tells the Thessalonians that preparation for the coming of the Lord is nothing more or less than faithful living in response to the gospel. At the coming of the Lord, what is now hidden in history under the sign of the cross will be brought to full realization, so that the hope of salvation will become the consummation of salvation. To speculate about the time of the coming of the Lord is irrelevant, for the Lord will come in love to do love's work, to give faithful people life with God forever. This vision of the final victory of love inspires Paul to close his advice on this subject with these words: "Therefore encourage one another and build each other up, just as in fact you are doing" (5:11).

■ **1 Thessalonians 5:12-22.** These final instructions have to do with church order and discipline. Since the church is a human community, its corporate life requires orderly supervision and efficient administration. These are not ends in themselves. Rather, they are means to peace and to the care of the congregation. Persons are due respect and honor in the church, not because of the office they hold, but because of the service they render. All, whether in leadership roles or in supportive roles, come under the same mandates: to live in peace, to be patient with all, to "strive to do what is good for each other and for everyone else," and to "rejoice always, pray continually, give thanks in all circumstances" (5:15-16). These are not simply words of practical wisdom; they are also the response that the call of God in Christ Jesus demands of the church.

Paul's understanding of the church, however, is not institutional but spiritual. The Spirit creates the church and equips it with the gifts needed for its existence. Therefore, Paul warns the church not to allow organizational concerns to quench the Spirit. But the gifts of the Spirit are to be tested by the message the church has received about Jesus Christ. What meets that standard is to be conserved as good; everything that fails is to be rejected as evil.

■ **1 Thessalonians 5:23-28.** Paul comes to the close of this letter with a final benediction, a request for prayer, a greeting for the brethren, instruction about circulating the letter, and a farewell. Just as he had earlier dealt with problems of doctrine and conduct in the context of his faith in God, so in these concluding verses Paul's unshakable confidence in God comes fully to voice. The future of the church is guaranteed, not because of Paul's ministry or because of the faithfulness of the Thessalonians, but because God, who calls the church into existence, is faithful. God will provide all that the church needs to live in peace and holiness now and to stand "blameless at the coming of our Lord Jesus Christ" (5:23). Since Paul lives out of this assurance of God's love, Paul's relationship with the saints is characterized by receiving love from them and offering love to them as signs of their common experiences of grace.

DIMENSION THREE: WHAT DOES THE BIBLE MEAN TO ME?

1 Thessalonians 4:13-18—The Coming of the Lord

How may the modem Christian find relevant meaning in Paul's faith in the coming of the Lord? Paul uses imagery he inherited from first-century Judaism when he writes of the coming of the Lord. The imagery, taken from observable human realities, is used to talk or write about unobservable divine realities. The important thing to keep in mind is not the form of the imagery but the substance of the message. What meaning can we receive from the imagery that applies to our lives?

1. Paul's faith in the coming of the Lord expresses his conviction that in Jesus Christ, God's final purpose for the salvation of the whole creation has already been revealed and put in action.

2. The coming of the Lord is necessary because what has been revealed and initiated is only imperfectly realized in the life of the church.

3. The coming of the Lord enlarges the realm of redemption to include not only the church but the whole creation.

4. The coming of the Lord encourages the church to persist in its ministry and assures the church that its life in the Lord has ultimate meaning.

How are these ideas relevant for you in your Christian life? What other dimensions of Paul's teachings about the coming of the Lord are particularly helpful to you?

1 Thessalonians 5:1-11—
Preparation for the Lord's Coming

Attempts persist to establish a timetable for the end. The preoccupation with chronology seems to arise from a deep-seated human need to be in control. If we know when, then we will know what to do. How do you feel about Christians who are sure that certain signs in contemporary history are clues for setting the date for the coming of the Lord? On the basis of Paul's teaching, what is the proper response to such claims?

Paul's positive instruction about preparation for the coming of the Lord is to live now as if the end has already come. What does this mean in our situation as we prepare for the coming of the Lord? Consider these suggestions:

1. Make every decision an opportunity for serving the Lord.

2. Resist attitudes and actions in our lives and in the world that deny the lordship of Christ.

3. Persist in the struggle against evil because the victory of the Lord is assured.

4. Live in hope for all the world because God in Christ loves all the world.

5. Live in confident self-giving because self-giving is the ultimate power of God.

The only preparation for the coming of the Lord is to live a faithful life in response to what God has done, is doing, and will do to redeem the whole creation. If you knew for sure that the end would come in the next few minutes, what would you do? In what sense is the coming of the Lord always a surprise? In what sense will it be a surprise only for those who reject the Lord? In what sense can you say that it will be no surprise to those who live the life of faith? What does the coming of the Lord require of you?

*Now may the Lord of peace himself give you peace at all times
and in every way. The Lord be with all of you. (3:16)*

7

CHRISTIAN LIFE BETWEEN THE TIMES

2 Thessalonians

DIMENSION ONE: WHAT DOES THE BIBLE SAY?

Answer these questions by reading 2 Thessalonians 1

1. Of what does Paul boast? (1:4)

2. For what do the Thessalonians suffer? (1:5)

3. To what end does Paul pray for the Thessalonians? (1:11)

Answer these questions by reading 2 Thessalonians 2

4. Who must come before the Lord comes? (2:3)

5. Who does the "man of lawlessness" proclaim himself to be? (2:4)

6. Who will overthrow and destroy the lawless one? (2:8)

7. How will the lawless one come? (2:9-10)

8. Why does Paul give thanks? (2:13)

9. To what are the Thessalonians to hold? (2:15)

10. Who will encourage their hearts "and strengthen [them] in every good deed and word"? (2:16-17)

Answer these questions by reading 2 Thessalonians 3

11. For what does Paul request prayer? (3:1-2)

12. Who is faithful? (3:3)

13. What will the Lord do? (3:3)

14. In whom does Paul have confidence? (3:4)

15. What does Paul tell the idle to do? (3:12)

16. What are the Thessalonians to do to anyone who refuses to obey what Paul says in this letter? (3:14)

DIMENSION TWO: WHAT DOES THE BIBLE MEAN?

■ **2 Thessalonians 1:1-2.** These verses of salutation and greeting reproduce almost word for word the opening verses of First Thessalonians. The commentary on those verses is sufficient for understanding what Paul is seeking to say here about his relationship to the Thessalonians and theirs to him (see lesson 5, page 42).

■ **2 Thessalonians 1:3-4.** When Paul thinks of the church, he always thinks of what God has done, is doing, and will do to create a community of faith in the world. The marks of the church, a people growing in faith and increasing in love, are the signs of God's power to accomplish God's saving purpose in human history. Therefore, the reality of the church in Thessalonica does not prompt Paul to flatter the brothers and sisters, nor is it the occasion for self-congratulations; rather, it is an inspiration to give thanks to God. Thanksgiving is Paul's characteristic activity because it expresses the fact of God's absolute dependability in all human experience. In the midst of the ebb and flow of human history, the unchanging center of the life of the church is God's self-giving love revealed in Jesus Christ. Since that love never fails, Paul is bound to give thanks always.

One distinctive form of apostolic thanksgiving is boasting. *Boast* is a favorite word of Paul's because it indicates that dependence on God is not a timid retreat from the challenges and assaults of the world but a world-confronting pledge of allegiance to God in open defiance of every rival to God's reign. Paul's boasting is a radical reversal of the world's boasting. By boasting, Paul witnesses to his obedience to God in confident faith, whereas the world's boasting is rebellion against God in anxious self-service. This radical reversal is seen here in the fact that Paul boasts, not because the saints at Thessalonica are enjoying worldly success, but rather because they are steadfast and faithful in the midst of all the persecutions and afflictions they are enduring. Paul's boasting calls attention to the faithfulness of the Thessalonians as evidence that God's final victory over evil is already present in human history. Although they are exposed to persecution and trials in the world, no hostile power is able to overcome them because God sustains them.

■ **2 Thessalonians 1:5-12.** One resource that sustains the church in time of persecution and affliction is the hope that the Lord will come. At that time, the persecuted church will be rewarded by God because the community has been made worthy by taking part in the suffering of the kingdom under attack, to receive the kingdom in triumph. But those who do not know the true and living God revealed in Jesus and who disobey God's will as revealed in the self-giving love of Jesus, will experience the coming of the Lord as vengeance. The vivid details of the Lord coming "from heaven in blazing fire with his powerful angels" (1:7) are taken from imagery of the Last Judgment in first-century Jewish literature. The point of the imagery is that everything that is unloving will be destroyed by love, and everything that is born of love and sustained by love will be completed by love. Therefore, when love comes in the Lord of glory, everything that is unloving will be excluded from the Lord's presence.

All this is not abstract speculation for Paul; it is confidence that those who have served Christ in affliction will share fully in his final glorious victory and be filled with awe at the revelation of Christ's invincible power. The participation of the saints in the coming of the Lord is not a work of magic. Rather, it is the result of Paul's faithful witness to the gospel that brought them to faith and sustains them in faith.

Paul's concern for the saints in persecution and trials is not that they will be delivered from suffering but that, in suffering, God will make them worthy of their call. They become worthy by trusting in God's power to complete what God has begun in them: "your every desire goodness and your every deed prompted by faith" (1:11). In other words, by the grace of God they are enabled to will and perform what is pleasing to God. The self-giving love of God in Christ is the power that brought them to faith, and it is the power that will bind them inseparably to Christ when he is revealed from heaven. Paul's confidence about the future is based solidly on his experience now of "the grace of our God and the Lord Jesus Christ" (1:12).

■ **2 Thessalonians 2:1-12.** Paul writes here to correct the notion that the day of the Lord has already fully come. This misunderstanding on the part of some was creating a disturbance in the life of the church. Paul says that no genuine letter from him supports such an idea. He goes on to state that before the day of the Lord comes fully, the following events must take place: (1) Rebellion of the forces of evil will break out. (2) The man of lawlessness, the son of perdition, will be loosed of all restraints and revealed as the one who exalts himself over all so-called gods and proclaims himself to be God in the temple of God. (3) "The Lord Jesus will overthrow [him] with the breath of his mouth and destroy [him] by the splendor of his coming" (2:8).

Once more, the imagery Paul uses to instruct the Thessalonians about the last things comes from Jewish literature, but the meaning he expresses in the imagery comes from his experience of Jesus Christ as the agent of God's saving purpose. On the basis of that experience, Paul makes the following statements about the end: (1) The opposition to Jesus, which resulted in his crucifixion, is the hidden rebellion of all the forces of evil and their idolatrous leader. (2) The salvation that Jesus has begun in the world will not be perfected until all the forces of rebellion and idolatry have been brought into the open and destroyed. (3) The power of evil and the attraction of idolatry have no real existence but are the illusions that are sustained by deceit. (4) Jesus has begun the overthrow of the realm of deception and delusion by confessing the truth and creating a community of those who are saved by the love of the truth. (5) The word of the truth, the gospel, which has begun the work of salvation among those who believe, is the reality that destroys the deceit of Satan, the lawless one, and all who believe what is false. So, although the end has not fully come, the end is already anticipated in those who hear the truth and believe, and in those who believe what is false and are destroyed.

Paul gave them this message when he first brought the gospel to Thessalonica. He reminds the saints of his basic message so that they will continue to depend on God to sustain them in the war against evil and not be lulled into a false sense of security by those who claim mistakenly that the final victory has already been accomplished.

■ **2 Thessalonians 2:13–3:5.** Now Paul returns to the themes of thanksgiving and intercession with which he began his letter. He is moved to give thanks by remembering that the saints are what they are because they are beloved by the Lord and chosen by God. These divine actions created the church in the beginning and destined it for the salvation that will be fully realized at the coming of the Lord. The Spirit set the church apart to be a holy community, sanctified by obedience to God's will and dependent on the truth revealed in Jesus. All this occurred in Thessalonica because the gospel was preached faithfully by Paul and will continue to happen there as long as the church stands firm and holds fast to the message he taught them by word of mouth and sends them now by letter.

Paul is moved to intercede for them with God, for he knows that no human power can sustain them in the struggle against wicked deception and strong delusion. He commends them to God, not as a last resort, but as the beginning and end of their faith in the Lord Jesus Christ. The self-giving love of God is the grace that assures them of eternal comfort and good hope. That self-same love empowers them to persevere in witnessing to the lordship of Christ "in every good deed and word."

What Paul knows about the Thessalonians he also knows about himself. Therefore, he requests that they pray for him. His ministry of the word is impossible unless the Lord enables it to "spread rapidly and be honored" (3:1), in spite of those who are evil, wicked, and unfaithful. Paul's request for prayer brings him again to a bold statement of his confidence that God will be faithful in persecution. In the midst of all the conflicting powers of human history, Christ himself is present, revealing the love of God as the ruling center of the church and the world.

■ **2 Thessalonians 3:6-15.** Paul turns to another theme in these closing verses. Paul instructs the community to avoid those who are idle. Idleness is probably lifted up here because it is a blatant form of self-indulgence that contradicts Paul's message of self-giving love. Paul's appeal to his teaching and to his example of working to support himself is offered as a corrective to those who are living in idleness: "They are not busy; they are busybodies" (3:11). Although Paul had the right to be supported as an apostle, he gave up that right for the welfare of the community. The full force of his argument is directed toward members of the community who have publicly assumed responsibility for their brothers and sisters but are now neglecting their duty. He reminds them of his earlier teaching: "The one who is unwilling to work shall not eat" (3:10). Then he commands them to change their ways, and instructs the community to shun all who disobey his orders, not as enemies to be punished, but as brothers and sisters to be shamed into reformation.

■ **2 Thessalonians 3:16-18.** The concluding benediction invokes the peace of God—the welfare that God bestows freely on all—as the key to peaceful relationships within the community. The Lord's abiding presence with them all, the idle and disorderly as well as the quietly diligent, is the reality that makes possible community discipline and reform. Since Paul is aware that letters have been circulated falsely over his name, he puts his own personal mark on this letter to assure all that this instruction is his.

DIMENSION THREE: WHAT DOES THE BIBLE MEAN TO ME?

2 Thessalonians 1:2; 3:16—The Peace of God

Peace in the context of biblical faith is never just the absence of conflict but the full realization of God's saving purpose for all creation. Through faith, the church enjoys the foretaste of God's peace now. How is this view different from our ordinary understanding of *peace*? Do you find it appealing or threatening?

How have you experienced God's peace? How can we show that we have received the peace of God? How can we really enjoy God's peace unless we are willing to forgive others as God has forgiven us? How does peacemaking make one vulnerable to suffering, to affliction, and to persecution? Name some instances of peacemaking that have involved the church in conflict with the world.

Some attitudes and actions in our world hinder the total welfare of all God's children, such as selfishness, prejudice, fear, injustice, sexism, ageism, and racism. Knowing that peace is not a passive absence of conflict, but an active bringing of the kingdom of God, does our invoking the peace of God at the close of our worship services carry with it our commitment to expose and conquer these attitudes and actions? How can we respond to the peace of God we invoke each week?

God's method of establishing peace on earth is self-giving love. This love is experienced as judgment by those who reject it and as grace by those who accept it. Does this mean that when we reject God's peace, we experience wrath or punishment? Are those messengers of God who disturb us the most also the most effective ministers of peace in our lives? Does God answer our prayers for peace by sending us prophets and teachers who shatter our peace? How was Jesus such a messenger?

2 Thessalonians 3:6-15—Discipline in the Church

What is the purpose of church discipline? Is it ever permissible to discipline in order to punish? What is the norm for evaluating any specific disciplinary action in the church? Is it possible to use cruel and destructive discipline in the name of our Lord Jesus Christ? How do you think Paul's teaching on church discipline reflects the self-giving love of Christ?

Is it possible that our tolerance is not an expression of Christian love but rather of not caring for the welfare of the community? Do we often refuse to hold others to high standards because we do not want to be held accountable ourselves? How can we be genuinely concerned for the welfare of others and at the same time refuse to confront them when they hold opinions and engage in activities that we deem destructive?

Keep in mind here that Paul is not advising the church to withdraw from the world. His point is that faith in Christ always results in a distinctive manner of life. When this is not evident in the church, the gospel is being rejected, and the church is threatened. What is the distinctive life of the church? Is this life manifest in us? How can we begin to correct the situation?

Here is a trustworthy saying that deserves full acceptance:
Christ Jesus came into the world to save sinners. (1:15)

8

CHRIST FOR ALL

1 Timothy 1–2

DIMENSION ONE:
WHAT DOES THE BIBLE SAY?

Answer these questions by reading 1 Timothy 1

1. Who writes the letter to whom? (1:1-2)

2. Where did Paul leave Timothy? (1:3)

3. What is the goal of Paul's command? (1:5)

4. For whom is law made? (1:9-10)

5. How had Paul acted? (1:13)

6. Why did Christ Jesus come into the world? (1:15)

7. Who is the worst sinner? (1:15-16)

8. What was Paul shown? (1:16)

9. Who are among those who "have suffered shipwreck with regard to the faith"? (1:19b-20)

10. To whom has Paul handed them? Why? (1:20)

Answer these questions by reading 1 Timothy 2

11. For whom should "petitions, prayers, intercession and thanksgiving be made"? (2:1)

12. Whom does God our Savior want to be saved? (2:3-4)

13. Who is the "one mediator between God and mankind"? (2:5)

14. How are women to learn? (2:11)

15. Does Paul permit women to teach or have authority over men? (2:12)

DIMENSION TWO: WHAT DOES THE BIBLE MEAN?

■ **1 Timothy 1:1-2.** Once more Paul uses the conventions of first-century letter writing to identify himself, the one whom he addresses, and the experience that binds them together. Paul is an apostle of Christ Jesus, sent to represent Christ. The authority he exercises comes from his orders from God and from Christ Jesus.

Timothy is identified by his relationship to Paul's message. He is a "true son in the faith" (1:2). This phrase does not refer to Paul's age and to Timothy's youth but rather acknowledges that the authority of the gospel message is the power that, in the preaching of Paul, brings forth Timothy's faithful obedience. Paul and Timothy participate in the peace of God in the only way open to sinful persons: through the grace and mercy of God given to them in Christ Jesus our Lord.

■ **1 Timothy 1:3-7.** Paul's charge to Timothy emphasizes Timothy's responsibility at Ephesus to maintain the integrity of Paul's message against false teaching. Since the gospel message is the love of God in Christ, the proper response "is love, which comes from a pure heart and a good conscience and a sincere faith" (1:5). False teaching that seeks to replace the gospel message with myths, endless genealogies, controversies, and meaningless talk is denounced as swerving away from "God's work—which is by faith" (1:4).

■ **1 Timothy 1:8-11.** It appears from these verses that one of the mistaken notions advanced by "some" (1:6) at Ephesus was the idea that the gospel of God's self-giving love in Christ needed to be supplemented by the law. Paul argues that the law has only one purpose: to restrain the lawless and disobedient. In that sense, the law is necessary for order in a sinful world. But the law has no binding force for those who accept Christ Jesus as Lord. Those who insist that salvation depends on ethical or liturgical works of the law are false teachers, who "do not know what they are talking about or what they so confidently affirm" (1:7). Sound doctrine, however, consists of holding fast "the gospel concerning the glory of the blessed God" (1:11) with which Paul has been entrusted. Those who live in response to the gospel have no need for the law and its works because, in the power of the gospel, they have left the company of immoral persons and all others who fail to love and entered the community of God's faithful children.

■ **1 Timothy 1:12-17.** Paul's greatest asset in the struggle against false teaching is not his brilliant argument but his experience of "the gospel concerning the glory of the blessed God" (1:11). Paul's thought is controlled by the gift of strength that enables him to serve Christ Jesus. He did nothing to earn Christ's favor, but is judged faithful by Christ in spite of the fact that he blasphemed and persecuted and insulted Christ. The pivotal word in the passage is *but*, for it indicates the radical reversal in Paul's life that brought him from the rebellion of disobedience to the faith of obedience. He deserved God's wrath and punishment; instead, he received God's mercy.

Remember that Paul's life before Christ was not degenerate and immoral but upright and scrupulously correct, morally and liturgically. Yet Paul denounces his previous knowledge of God as ignorance and his prior life of obedience as unbelief. Everything he sought to earn from God simply brought him deeper alienation from God. He rejected God and deserved rejection in turn. But God did not reject him. In Christ, Paul was claimed by God for God's service, not grudgingly but freely, as grace overflowed in his life, producing in him faith and love.

The source of sound doctrine is mercy and grace. The gospel is God's action on behalf of sinners. The notion that God requires something from sinners before God saves them is the root of all false teaching. Whatever it may be, knowledge or conduct or a combination, is erroneous because it makes salvation dependent on human achievement rather than a work of God's mercy and grace. Such teaching is unsure and unworthy of acceptance because it limits salvation to an exclusive group. Here Paul answers the lie with the truth: "Here is a trustworthy saying that deserves full acceptance: Christ Jesus came into the world to save sinners" (1:15). God's action in Christ Jesus is absolutely final in the sense that nothing more remains to be done. It is absolutely inclusive in the sense that no one is disqualified.

As an apostle, Paul had a unique responsibility in the church; but he had no special status in relationship to Christ Jesus. Paul received salvation as a sinner. His reputation as a sinner serves only to highlight the mercy in which all sinners stand before Christ. Paul is an example, not of human achievement, but of the perfect patience of God. God's patience is extended to all sinners so that they might turn from the rebellion that leads to destruction to the faith that leads to eternal life.

In the conflict with false teachers at Ephesus, what was at stake was not Paul's honor and glory but the honor and glory of God. God's honor is established in the fact that God's saving purpose was revealed in Jesus Christ. Salvation is no longer an illusion but a reality that has come into human history in Christ and is available now through faith in Christ. God's glory is the self-giving love of God that is victorious over sin and death in the cross and resurrection of Jesus. Wherever the faithful share in Jesus Christ's suffering, they enter into the glory of his victory. So the doxology that comes as the climax to Paul's personal witness is his pledge of allegiance to the truth in defiance of all false teachers who dishonor God by glorifying themselves (1:17).

■ **1 Timothy 1:18-20.** Now Paul returns to the specific issue that prompted him to write to Timothy: instruction on how to resist false doctrine. The autobiographical notes in 1:12-17 point away from Paul to the action of God in Christ, and suggest that only in dependence on the truth (the gospel) can the lies (false doctrine) be withstood. Timothy was ordained for the struggle. The prophetic utterances that singled Timothy out for leadership in the church also equipped him to "fight the battle well" (1:18). But the military imagery is transformed by the strategy that Paul recommends. The threat is no longer from without but from within, and the weapons are no longer human power and guile but "faith and a good conscience" (1:19). What Timothy has to fear most is, not the liars, but that he will become a liar by depending on himself and sacrificing the integrity of his good conscience by seeking to save himself.

Hymenaeus and Alexander are mentioned as examples of persons who have shipwrecked their faith by rejecting conscience. Their failure was that, in seeking to save themselves, they destroyed themselves; and in resisting liars, they became liars themselves. Paul's turning them over to Satan seems harsh, but may be nothing more than acknowledging that human life is destroyed or saved by the object of its trust. At any rate, Paul's curse is not final but corrective, and has as its goal the reformation of those who have blasphemed by seeking to save themselves.

■ **1 Timothy 2:1-7.** This section takes up the theme of God's universal salvation that has already been hinted at in 1:1, by referring to God as "our Savior" and in 1:15, by declaring that "Christ Jesus came into the world to save sinners." Now the theme is developed more fully, as Paul tells Timothy—and through him the church—that "petitions, prayers, intercession and thanksgiving be made for everyone" (2:1). This is not simply the diplomatic thing for a minority group to do to win favor but a public witness to the sovereign reign of God that includes those who rule as well as those who are ruled. The prayers of the church for all are evidence that the church lives out of faith in God, and in that relationship with God, the church is sustained as a community that seeks to "live peaceful and quiet lives in all godliness and holiness" (2:2).

This action is good in the absolute sense because it is rooted and grounded in the saving purpose of God revealed in Christ Jesus. Since God is the Savior not only of the church but of sinners, God desires all to be saved by receiving "knowledge of the truth" (2:3) through faith in Christ Jesus. This saving purpose of God is God's very nature, given to all God's children through the one man who reveals God's nature in doing God's will, giving "himself as a ransom for all people" (2:6). All come to the knowledge of the truth that saves from lies and deceit through the testimony of Jesus to God's saving purpose. The testimony of Jesus is continued in history by the testimony of Paul, Timothy, and all faithful witnesses to the truth.

Paul's affirmation of the universality of God's saving purpose in Christ's self-giving love is directed against false teachers. Maybe one part of false teaching in Ephesus was a withdrawal from contact with the world in order to concentrate on so-called higher revelations and holier conduct that would save the church from the destruction that was falling on all who were outside the community. Those who think this way are not telling the truth; they are lying. But Paul, in his ministry to the Gentiles, tells the truth. He is not lying, for his message proclaims the truth revealed in the cross of Jesus Christ. He charges Timothy and the church to overcome the falsehood and lying of self-seeking idolatry by giving themselves in faithful ministry to all persons in obedience to God.

■ **1 Timothy 2:8-15.** In these verses, Paul lays down rules for public worship that are motivated and controlled by his concern that the church be a community witnessing to God's saving purpose for all the world. Public worship at Ephesus seems to have degenerated into something of a public spectacle, so that the function of the church as a witness to the gospel is being jeopardized by anger and quarreling, by women breaking the conventions of society in dress, and by women aggressively assuming leadership in the community. Paul seeks to counter this by urging women to conform to the standards of good taste in matters of clothes and to obey what he understands as God's law in matters of status and role in worship.

Neither Paul's strategy nor his arguments are particularly convincing to the modern reader. We must remember Paul was writing with specific issues in mind and spoke from a perspective conditioned by the historical and cultural circumstances in which he lived. Knowing the context, we can more easily understand the point Paul is teaching and its relevancy for us today. The worship of the Ephesians was drawing attention away from its message, the message of the gospel. Here, his concern that the church do nothing in public worship to hinder its evangelizing work in the world can be affirmed.

DIMENSION THREE: WHAT DOES THE BIBLE MEAN TO ME?

1 Timothy 2:5-6—Christ Jesus as a Ransom for All

Do you experience sin as bondage to a power greater than yourself? Is this a common human experience? What evidences in our personal and social life seem to result from bondage to sin? How would acceptance of the imagery of Christ as the one who ransoms all from sin's power change our understanding of ourselves? How would it change our understanding of others? Does it change the way we think about God and Christ?

Do we often live as if we have no need for God? Is this *independence* sin? How does this basic sin of independence express itself in sin or sinful acts?

The imagery of Christ as a ransom for all helps us experience God's love as the purpose of God for our laws and for all. Is this good news for you? Have you tried to tell others of this good news? How is this good news expressed in the worship and work of the church?

1 Timothy 2:8-15—The Status and Role of Women in the Church

Most Christians today do not follow Paul's teaching about apparel for women and the subordination of women in public worship. What really motivated Paul? Were his concerns legitimate? Is it possible to accept Paul's intent while rejecting his specific teachings?

Can the church carry out its evangelistic work while denying women full access to positions of leadership and responsibility in the church? What has been the impact of the ordination of women as pastors and the placement of women as leaders on the evangelistic task of the church? What responsibility does the church have to work toward full access to economic, legal, and political activity for women in society?

I am writing you these instructions so that, if I am delayed, you will know how people ought to conduct themselves in God's household. (3:14-15)

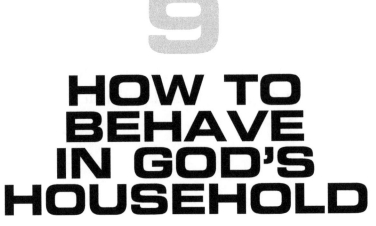

HOW TO BEHAVE IN GOD'S HOUSEHOLD

1 Timothy 3–4

DIMENSION ONE: WHAT DOES THE BIBLE SAY?

Answer these questions by reading 1 Timothy 3

1. What kind of task is the office of overseer (bishop)? (3:1)

2. What kind of person must an overseer be, and what must an overseer manage well? (3:2, 4)

3. Who must think well of an overseer? (3:7)

4. What must deacons hold with a clear conscience? (3:9)

5. What must their wives be? (3:11)

6. What do those who serve well as deacons gain? (3:13)

7. What does Paul hope to do? (3:14)

8. How does Paul describe the church? (3:15)

Answer these questions by reading 1 Timothy 4

9. How will some abandon the faith? (4:1)

10. What is good? (4:4)

11. What is Timothy to train himself to be? (4:7b)

12. For what does godliness hold promise? (4:8)

13. Who is "the Savior of all people"? (4:10)

14. For whom is Timothy urged to set an example? (4:12)

15. What does Paul charge Timothy to devote himself to? (4:13)

16. Whom will Timothy save by watching his life and doctrine closely? (4:16)

DIMENSION TWO: WHAT DOES THE BIBLE MEAN?

■ **1 Timothy 3:1-7.** Here Paul instructs Timothy about the character of those who aspire to administrative functions in the church. The focus of attention is not on the office but on the qualifications one must have for the office. These qualifications are essential because the office of overseer or administrator (or bishop) is not an end in itself but rather a means to an end: the care of God's church.

Therefore, to set one's heart "to be an overseer" (3:1) is not a worldly ambition but a response to God's call to service. God's call to service is the radical reorientation of life that always accompanies the hearing of the gospel: dying with Christ to self and rising with Christ to life for others. The office of overseer is a life for others. Paul's instruction to Timothy about the character of overseers in these verses reminds the church that the management of the household of God can be done only in the power of the gospel. In these verses, that power comes to voice so that the church will not lack faithful and efficient administrators.

These verses may reveal a crisis in the church created by self-seeking persons within the ranks of those charged with the care of God's church. The fact that temperance, self-control, respectability, hospitality, and gentleness are emphasized may reveal that scandals of drunkenness, violence, quarrelsomeness, and greed had broken out among the managers of the household of God. If that was the case, then Paul is calling them to repentance by confronting them once again with the power of the gospel, and by warning them of the condemnation and ruin that will surely result from failing to hear his message.

■ **1 Timothy 3:8-13.** The focus is not on the office of deacon but on the character of those who fill the office. Although it is usually assumed that the office of overseer is superior to that of deacon, nothing in the text warrants that assumption. The primary concern is that only those who have been tested and found worthy be permitted to serve the church as deacons. Paul gives no indication of who will do the testing. He insists only that the testing must be done to secure blameless persons for service as deacons.

In this context, sound doctrine and correct behavior are not two different things. They are the inseparable components of an integrated and whole response to the gospel. Also, sound doctrine and correct behavior are not static possessions or achievements but a dynamic process of hearing and obeying the gospel. The character of deacons is developed, not by a regimen of self-discipline, but by a self-transcending commitment to the revelation of God's love in Christ. The text is much more than it seems to be, for it presupposes the action of God in Christ as the norm for serving well as deacons and the power that makes that norm operative in the life of the church.

Perhaps the key to interpreting this whole section is given in 3:9: "They must keep hold of the deep truths of the faith with a clear conscience." The phrase "deep truths" does not mean a riddle or puzzle but the revelation of God's saving purpose in Christ. Only by holding to the truth revealed in the cross and resurrection of Christ Jesus can deacons serve well, earn a good reputation, and develop confidence to perform their tasks.

The text addresses real problems in the church: deacons who are frivolous, insincere, alcoholic, and greedy. Paul also sets before the church the possibility of reform by calling those who have failed the test to prove themselves blameless by hearing and obeying the gospel. The passage derives its life-changing power, not from Paul's specific exhortations, but from the action of God in Christ that always calls the church to repentance and renewal. The text speaks of what deacons must be and must do, not because of Paul's apostolic authority, but because of what God is and does. Since God is one in the promise and fulfillment of salvation, deacons must live out of that salvation by witnessing to it in acts of loving service.

■ **1 Timothy 3:14-16.** Paul's ministry is not limited to the places of his physical presence or to the times of his historical presence; it is extended in space and time by his written words of instruction. This letter, which is addressed to Timothy, is intended for the whole church. The motivation for the letter is practical rather than speculative. Paul writes so that the readers of his letter may know how they "ought to conduct themselves in God's household" (3:15).

What Paul has written about the character of overseers and deacons is instruction about conduct or behavior in "the church of the living God" (3:15). The church, as the household of God, is God's creation and exists in the world as a community for spreading and preserving the truth. The truth is personal in the sense that it is the mystery or revelation of God's love in Christ that is confessed in the gathered family of God. Where the truth of God is publicly acknowledged and publicly served, there is "God's household . . . the church of the living God."

Overseers, deacons, and the whole membership exist for one purpose only: to be "the pillar and foundation of the truth" (3:15). The content of the truth is summarized in the liturgical language of verse 16. As the rhythm and parallelism of the phrases suggest, this is poetry and is intended as a symbol of the truth rather than a literal definition. The entire verse is a confession of the faithful response of the community to the life, death, resurrection, and ascension of Jesus Christ. The revelation of the truth includes Jesus' life in the flesh, his resurrection from the dead by the power of the Spirit, and his ascension to a position of power among the angels. This message has been proclaimed among the nations and has created a faithful response in the world. This word of truth creates and sustains the church, and gives the church its reason for being.

The truth is not the creation of the church. Rather, the church is the creation of the truth. The truth is the norm of the church's life and the standard against which overseers, deacons, and all the members are judged. Only in holding the truth with single-minded devotion is the church protected from false doctrine and immoral action. The truth, the action of God in Jesus Christ, not only contains instruction about how the church ought to behave; it also releases, within those who hold it with a clear conscience, the power to serve well in the household of God.

■ **1 Timothy 4:1-5.** Paul denounces any departure from the truth, as summarized in 3:16, as the work of those powers that oppose God: deceitful spirits and demons. Those who turn away from the truth revealed in Jesus are the enemies of God. They are the ones who have departed from the living God to serve the false gods of their own deceit and illusion.

The specific false doctrines attacked in this passage are celibacy and abstinence from certain foods. These are denounced as coming "through hypocritical liars" (4:2) because they are a rejection of the good gifts of God to humankind. God has given sexual desire and hunger for food to men and women to enjoy in the discipline of thanksgiving and prayer. To refuse these good gifts is to turn away from God and dependence on God, and to seek to live without God, depending on one's own ascetic exercises.

The basic error attacked in these verses is the notion that the created world is evil, and that salvation consists in being delivered from the material world through abstention from marriage and certain foods. The view presented here as true is that nothing in creation is evil in itself, but is made evil by selfish and indulgent use. Salvation, according to these verses, consists in turning away from self to God in dependence on God's love. A sign of that dependence is a life of obedience to God in the disciplined enjoyment of all that God gives: marriage, food, every created thing. Salvation does not deliver one from the material world. Rather, salvation enables one to receive the material world as God's good gift to humankind.

■ **1 Timothy 4:6-10.** Paul reminds Timothy that just as overseers and deacons and the whole church are empowered to serve well by holding to the truth revealed in Jesus, so Timothy's ministry depends on the nourishment he receives by following "the truths of the faith and of the good teaching" (4:6). Timothy's ministry is not a matter of formal skills but of hearing and obeying the gospel. He is required to be on guard against the "godless myths and old wives' tales" (4:7) of those false teachers who make salvation dependent on celibacy and abstinence from foods.

What is required of "a good minister of Christ Jesus" (4:6) is nothing more than is required of all members of the household of God: training in godliness. Here Paul uses the metaphor of athletic training to suggest the valuable discipline of a godly life. Athletic training, since it has value only for the discipline of the body in this life, is far less valuable than training in godliness that prepares one to live responsibly before God in "both the present life and the life to come" (4:8). The emphasis on training in godliness is on the cultivation of the primary relationship of trust in God, which is the source, the nourishment, and the fulfillment of human existence.

The toiling and striving of the godly life are not ends in themselves. Rather, they are the result of hope centered in the living God. This hope arises from the fact that God is revealed in Jesus Christ as the Savior of all persons. However, universal salvation comes to full realization only in those who believe, who hear and obey the gospel.

■ **1 Timothy 4:11-16.** Training in godliness is given specific content in these instructions to Timothy. This entire section is a summary of all that has been developed in chapters 1–4. This concluding statement stresses once again the fundamental nature of Christian life as an integrated and complete response to the revelation of God's love in Jesus Christ. Since God is fully active in the gospel, only the response of the whole life of the believer is acceptable.

The authority of ministry arises in the first place from "these things" (4:11), that is, from the revealed truth. Maturity in ministry is not a matter of chronological age but of fulfilling the purpose of God in the daily routines of speech and conduct. Ministry in this context is not so much an ecclesiastical function as it is a total way of life. The essential marks of a good minister are the distinctive marks of Christian life: love, faith, and purity. Timothy is urged to demonstrate these characteristics by holding fast to the truth that operates in the life of the community by "the public reading of Scripture" (4:13) and by the interpretation and application of Scripture through preaching and teaching.

Timothy has been ordained to these duties in the household of God, but his maturity in them is not automatic. The gift of a responsible office in the church must always be claimed in diligent devotion to duty. This gift can be neglected and forfeited. Therefore, full appropriation of the gift of ministry always depends on disciplined devotion to the truth, the gospel of Jesus Christ. Only in the power of the gospel do ministers receive their salvation, and only in the power of the gospel are they made instruments of the salvation that God offers to all in Christ.

DIMENSION THREE: WHAT DOES THE BIBLE MEAN TO ME?

1 Timothy 3:14-16—How to Behave in God's Household

We often pride ourselves on caring little or nothing about what one believes because we are preoccupied with how one behaves. Is this attitude present in your church? Do you support it? What are some reasons for supporting this attitude? What are some reasons for questioning it?

A central emphasis of 1 Timothy is that the church is God's household. Among other things, this emphasis means that the church is God's creation, belongs to God, and takes its orders from God. Do you believe this doctrine? What implications does this doctrine have for how one ought to behave in the church?

A fundamental problem in the modern church is a lack of agreement on how one ought to behave in God's household. Perhaps a productive solution would be to seek to agree on what we believe about the church and then develop a consensus on behavior based on shared belief. For example, agreement that the church is God's household is the basis for a racially integrated church. What other examples of the relationship between what one believes about the church and how one behaves in the church can you think of? How do these examples support the view that indifference about what we believe in the church is the root cause of differences about how we ought to behave in the church?

1 Timothy 4:6-16—Qualifications of a Good Minister of Christ Jesus

We expect our ordained ministers to be competent in a wide range of functions. One problem of this expectation is that it puts ordained ministers under pressure to respond to all the needs of a complex institution. What functions do you expect your ordained ministers to perform? Do you evaluate their performance? What do they seem to do well? What do they appear to do poorly? Do you value some functions more highly than others? Why?

Often the expectations of a congregation are so diverse and so demanding that the resources of even the most dedicated and disciplined clergy are depleted and exhausted. Does the emphasis on training in godliness in First Timothy speak to this issue? Is a prerequisite for effective or quality ministry as laity or clergy a disciplined and devoted relationship to God in Christ? How can laity and clergy support and encourage one another in developing this relationship? Is it possible to persist in ministry as a layperson or as clergy without training in godliness?

For we brought nothing into the world, and we can take nothing out of it. But if we have food and clothing, we will be content with that. (6:7-8)

10

LIFE IN GOD'S HOUSEHOLD

1 Timothy 5–6

DIMENSION ONE: WHAT DOES THE BIBLE SAY?

Answer these questions by reading 1 Timothy 5

1. How is Timothy to treat older men, younger men, older women, and younger women? (5:1-2)

2. What happens to those who fail to provide for their relatives? (5:8)

3. At what age are widows to be enrolled? (5:9)

4. How many witnesses must testify to bring an accusation against an elder? (5:19)

5. What is to be done to elders who sin? (5:20)

6. Why is Timothy urged to take a little wine? (5:23)

7. How are good deeds described? (5:25)

Answer these questions by reading 1 Timothy 6

8. How are those under the yoke of slavery to consider their masters? (6:1)

9. In what is there great gain? (6:6)

10. What is a root of all kinds of evil? (6:10)

11. What is the "man of God" to pursue? (6:11)

12. Before whom did Christ Jesus in his testimony make "the good confession"? (6:13)

13. Who has seen the King of kings and Lord of lords? (6:15-16)

14. Who "richly provides us with everything for our enjoyment"? (6:17)

15. How have some wandered from the faith? (6:20-21)

DIMENSION TWO: WHAT DOES THE BIBLE MEAN?

■ **1 Timothy 5:1-2.** In these verses, Timothy, as one who has an administrative role in the household of God, is told to relate to those for whom he is responsible as if they were members of his family. The relationship he has to others because of their common allegiance to Christ requires that he treat them with dignity and respect. Therefore, he must not rebuke them, which means that his authority as a servant prohibits the use of violent or harsh words of discipline. As their minister, Timothy is committed to seeking their welfare. In their weakness and failure he is to speak words of admonition and comfort to them. Once more, it is clear that, although the management of the affairs of the household of God is patterned after the structure of contemporary society, it is motivated and empowered by the gospel, the revelation of God's self-giving love in Jesus Christ.

■ **1 Timothy 5:3-16.** This passage tells of a crisis in the life of the church in Asia. It appears that the resources of the church were being strained by enrolling as full-time church workers too many widows who depended on the church for their only support. The solution to the problem is two-pronged:

1. Only those who are "real" widows are to be enrolled. Only widows who have no relatives can become dependents of the church. All other widows are to be supported by their families, the accepted pattern in the society at large and the normal behavior of all believers. Failure to care for one's widowed relatives is irresponsible behavior in the household of God and falls below the moral standards of the world.

2. Only widows who are sixty years of age or older and have shown their ability to serve the church are to be enrolled. Widows under sixty years of age are to remarry, because they are likely to break their vows of chastity and bring discredit to the church.

■ **1 Timothy 5:17-25.** The word *honor* is introduced again in this section that deals with the support and discipline of elders. From the context, we learn that all elders performed administrative functions in the church. They were *presiding* elders. But some were also preachers and teachers. The implication is that they were full-time workers in the church and thus dependent on the church for their full support. "Double honor" (5:17) means special respect and adequate support so that such full-time elders will be able to carry out their duties without the distractions of other jobs or anxiety for their physical needs. This point needed to be emphasized because, apparently, full-time workers were often considered less worthy than lay teachers and preachers who supported themselves by their labor. The text insists that those who give themselves to full-time service and perform their functions responsibly be accepted without prejudice and be paid accordingly. The sanction for this is not practical wisdom but revealed truth, as the appeal to Scriptures makes clear.

Since elders were administrators, they were in positions of power that could be abused and that exposed them to suspicion and criticism. Only those who were "worthy" (5:17) were to be honored and supported. They were to be protected against false charges of misconduct in office by requiring two or three witnesses to support the charges. Persistent misconduct called for public reprimand, so that administrators would know they were accountable to the whole congregation.

One peril of administrative office is the temptation to claim administrative privilege. To avoid this temptation, the church is strongly advised to discipline, without partiality, those who abuse power. The fact that this point is emphasized shows that some elders ruled in an unworthy manner without reprimand, and that others who were reprimanded were spared rigorous discipline. The church is warned not to administer discipline partially and leniently, because in so doing the church becomes guilty of the sin it has failed to punish. The most important safeguard for the abuse of power by administrators is to remove unfit persons and by careful screening of those who seek office.

Verse 23 points out that those who abstain from wine by drinking only water are jeopardizing their health. Wine is recommended here as a necessary medicine. Elders who are devoted to their duties in the household of God will not neglect their health by refusing to take the medicine that is available. Good administration presupposes the physical well-being of administrators.

The passage ends with an affirmation of faith in the moral integrity of human existence. It may seem now that the abuse of power by some persons goes undetected and unjudged, just as the responsible use of power by others is unrecognized and unrewarded. But ultimately, evil will be revealed for what it is and judged accordingly. The good now hidden will be brought to light and shown as it really is. So the church is freed to make its disciplinary judgments as responsibly as it can, knowing that the evil it does not detect and the good it fails to see will be revealed fully in the end.

■ **1 Timothy 6:1-2.** Once more slavery is discussed as an unchallenged social construct. But here, a reality is introduced into the social context that ultimately brings every institution under judgment. This reality also calls all persons to a new possibility, regardless of social status. The reality is "God's name and our teaching" (6:1) or the power of God and the gospel. The text does not address slaves in general but Christian slaves, those who have been claimed by the love of God revealed in Jesus Christ. Slaves became Christian, not apart from their historical circumstance, but in the relationships of their history. God's power transforms slaves in relationship to their masters, and enables them to witness to that power by honoring their masters for the sake of the gospel.

The terrible burden of slavery is not made less by becoming Christian. Rather, according to Paul, the burden is transformed, so that Christian slaves bear their burdens as a witness to the self-giving love of God revealed in Jesus Christ. This is especially true for slaves whose masters are Christian. Although masters and slaves are brothers and sisters in Christ, this relationship in the gospel does not nullify the duty of slaves to honor their masters. Instead, their duty is heightened because the service rendered is to be a believer and a beloved in the household of God.

■ **1 Timothy 6:3-5.** The key to right conduct in the household of God is right teaching, or the gospel of Jesus Christ that is faithfully transmitted by Paul and other ministers. The primary relationship of trust in God—godliness—is the source of all other responsible relationships among the members of the family. If that relationship is broken or replaced by the "godless myths and old wives' tales" (4:7) of false teachers, then the community loses its center, is split into competing and quarreling factions, and is led by self-serving charlatans whose greed dishonors the church and defames God. Right teaching always implies right action. Therefore, the whole gospel, as proclaimed by Paul in this letter to Timothy, is summed up in the words: "These are the things you are to teach and insist on" (6:2c).

■ **1 Timothy 6:6-10.** The discontent of those who teach and follow false doctrine is now contrasted with the contentment of those who teach and follow the truth. Their true gain, as contrasted with the false gain of perishable wealth, is their trust in God. This trust enables them to be content not only amid the changing fortunes of earthly existence but also in the face of the unknown mystery of life eternal. The desire to be rich is wrong and destructive. It turns men and women away from trust in God, traps them into seeking satisfaction from those things that only increase their discontent, and plunges them into insatiable longing for things beyond their grasp. The desire to be rich, the "love of money" (6:10), is the basic sin that separates men and women from God and from one another. Those who wander away from the faith by seeking contentment through wealth are doomed to suffer many griefs.

■ **1 Timothy 6:11-16.** This general teaching is now applied to Timothy. Timothy is directed to flee from "the love of money" by fixing his attention on those goals that give contentment because they reflect allegiance to God: "righteousness, godliness, faith, love, endurance and gentleness" (6:11). These goals are duties that arise from God's nature revealed in Jesus Christ. They are always goals, because human beings live in a world where God's saving purpose is under attack by those forces that deny God and claim the allegiance that belongs to God alone. The metaphor of "the good fight of the faith" (6:12) is used here to emphasize that faith is always a decision about ultimate loyalty, made in the crisis of conflicting centers of power: God or the world. The model Timothy is urged to follow as he confesses his allegiance to God is the good confession he made at his baptism. That model is not a human ideal but a divine commandment arising from the fact that God is the Creator of all life and Christ is the Redeemer.

Life is redeemed when one gives one's loyalty to God. This redemption is a human possibility because Christ Jesus "before Pontius Pilate made the good confession" (6:13) by giving himself completely to God. Since God is the Creator revealed in the redemptive obedience of Christ Jesus, Timothy is under orders to live in absolute dependence on God until the coming of Christ Jesus at the end. The power that motivates and sustains Timothy in fighting "the good fight of the faith" until the end is the invisible God, whose majesty and glory inspire Paul to burst forth into a breathtaking doxology (6:15-16). Because this God is revealed to Timothy in "the good confession" of Christ Jesus, Timothy himself is called to "take hold of the eternal life to which you were called" now by fighting "the good fight of the faith" (6:12).

■ **1 Timothy 6:17-19.** The vision of God contained in the doxology in the preceding verses humbles the rich, and confronts them with the fact that their only sure hope is God, whose grace richly provides the contentment that money can never buy. The duty of the rich is to live for others, to practice charity, and to be liberal and generous. The invisible God is honored by the rich as they conform to God's redemptive love by giving themselves for those under their authority. The visible relationships of their lives are the arena in which they must make their good confession and claim for themselves the gift of eternal life. To fail to use their wealth for the good of others is to defame God and the gospel.

■ **1 Timothy 6:20-21.** The letter concludes with a direction to Timothy and the whole church to hold fast to sound doctrine. The gospel that Paul preaches will conform them to itself and enable them to avoid the seductions and attractions of false teaching. Only in the gospel does the church know the truth, guard the truth, and avoid falsehood. So, as Paul comes to the end of this letter of instruction to those fighting "the good fight of the faith" in the household of God, his benediction reminds them that God who called them into the struggle sustains them to the end: "Grace be with you all" (6:21).

DIMENSION THREE: WHAT DOES THE BIBLE MEAN TO ME?

1 Timothy 5:17-25—The Remuneration and Discipline of Elders

What is adequate support for full-time ordained ministers? Is it the same for all, or should distinctions be made that justify different levels of support for different kinds of service? Should distinctions also be made on the basis of quality of service, so that those who excel would be paid more than those who are less effective?

Ordained ministers, because of their functions, are vulnerable to criticism and complaint. So they need to be protected from unwarranted charges and unfounded accusations. Are you aware of this in your church? What are some safeguards that can be used in your church to protect ordained ministers from false charges and criticism?

In the case of misconduct among ordained ministers, is discipline administered impartially and rigorously? At issue is not the gross forms of misconduct that would justify removal from office but those actions that harm the church and render the witness of the church ineffective. Are you inclined to ignore such things and be lenient about them when confronted with them? How does such indifference threaten the life of the household of God?

1 Timothy 6:12—The Warfare of Christian Existence

This verse seems to indicate that to be a believer in the gospel is to be engaged in a war against the enemies of God. Do you feel that God is calling you into a war against evil? Who is with you in the battle? What are God's weapons in the warfare? Do you have these weapons in your arsenal? How are you using them?

This verse also calls us to the "eternal life" to which we have been called. The grace that works within us before we make a decision to align our lives with God is called "prevenient grace." This verse seems to refer to such grace, that we are called to eternal life and then make our commitment to God as a result. "Your good confession in the presence of many witnesses" is the public pledge of allegiance to God that is part of the sacrament of baptism. In seeing our faith as a battle against God's enemies, one could interpret our baptism as the enlistment into that battle. Do you understand baptism in this way? Is a sign of our having eternal life now the fact that we are fighting "the good fight of the faith"? How do you fight the good fight of faith? Is the confession of allegiance to God a one-time event, or must it be made over and over again as our allegiance to God is challenged by other loyalties?

I have fought the good fight, I have finished the race, I have kept the faith. (4:7)

11
CHRISTIAN ENDURANCE

2 Timothy

DIMENSION ONE: WHAT DOES THE BIBLE SAY?

Answer these questions by reading 2 Timothy 1

1. Whom does Paul serve? (1:3)

2. What is Paul appointed? (1:11)

3. What is Timothy to guard? (1:14)

4. Who is not ashamed of Paul's chains? (1:16)

Answer these questions by reading 2 Timothy 2

5. In what is Timothy to be strong? (2:1)

6. What do Hymenaeus and Philetus say? (2:17b-18)

7. What produces quarrels? (2:23)

8. To whom must "the Lord's servant" be kind? (2:24)

Answer these questions by reading 2 Timothy 3

9. What comes in the last days? (3:1)

10. Who rescued Paul from persecutions and sufferings? (3:11)

11. Who will be persecuted? (3:12)

Answer these questions by reading 2 Timothy 4

12. Who is to judge the living and the dead? (4:1)

13. What is Timothy to preach? (4:2)

14. Who did "a great deal of harm" to Paul? (4:14)

DIMENSION TWO: WHAT DOES THE BIBLE MEAN?

■ **2 Timothy 1:1-2.** In union with Christ, Paul supervises the clergy, who are represented by Timothy. In union with Christ, the clergy recognize Paul's authority over them. The primary relationship, therefore, that controls the accountability of those set apart for ministry in the church is to Christ Jesus. In that relationship, all distinctions of rank and status are secondary. All share alike in the common experiences of grace, mercy, and peace that are the characteristic marks of life in the household of God.

■ **2 Timothy 1:3-7.** In these verses, Paul remembers Timothy's life as a means of setting before the clergy a pattern of behavior worthy of imitation. Memory, in this context, is centered, not on human achievement, but on the action of God in the lives of those called to service in the church. Therefore, Paul's memory of Timothy expresses itself in thanks to God.

Paul's experience of God's action is paralleled by Timothy's nurture in a Christian home, in the context of Timothy's family heritage. The relationship between Paul and Timothy is supported by a network of faithful persons, including Timothy's grandmother and mother. God's work is assured, not in vague generalities, but in the specific response of faithful men and women. The faith Timothy received in his home has been confirmed by his ordination to service in the church.

The gifts of God through family and ordination are not, however, automatic. Timothy and all the clergy represented by him must stir up the flame that has been kindled in them at ordination. If they neglect or take it for granted, it may burn low or even die out. They can keep the flame glowing by remembering and using the gifts they received at their ordination: "a spirit of power, love and self-discipline" (1:7). God's Spirit is at work in their spirits, endowing them with the energy, compassion, and discipline to persevere and transmit the faith, not timidly, but boldly and confidently.

■ **2 Timothy 1:8-14.** Boldness is necessary because loyal service to the crucified Lord entails suffering for the Lord's sake and for the gospel. This suffering is never hopeless and meaningless. This suffering is always in the power of God's self-giving love and always the means whereby that love is made known in the world. Just as we have no gospel without the action of God in the cross and resurrection of Christ Jesus, so no one preaches the gospel without the action of God's Holy Spirit in the suffering and endurance of those ordained to ministry. What enables Paul and all the clergy to endure until the coming of the Lord is the victory of Christ Jesus over death. This victory is a present reality in the faith and love of Timothy and all clergy. They are victorious in suffering because the Holy Spirit enables them to obey and guard what has been entrusted to them, the gospel.

■ **2 Timothy 1:15-18.** The reference to suffering is especially poignant, for it reminds Paul of how, in his imprisonment, he was abandoned by some and comforted by others. Faith and love are shown by ministers of the gospel in situations of critical human need, but not all meet the test. Some, like Phygelus and Hermogenes, were ashamed of Paul's suffering in prison. Others, like Onesiphorus, were not ashamed of Paul's chains. They sought him out, ministered to his needs, shared his shame, and exposed themselves and their families to the dangers that had befallen him. Since they were involved with Paul in his suffering, they are sustained now and will be sustained in the Day of Judgment by the mercy that comes from the Lord alone. Ordained ministers of the gospel guard the truth that has been entrusted to them, not by debating the truth, but by living it in circumstances that require them to suffer because of their allegiance to the truth. Onesiphorus is a model for all clergy to be witnesses to the gospel, not in words only, but in the "many ways he helped me in Ephesus" (1:28).

■ **2 Timothy 2:1-7.** All that Paul has written up to this point may be seen as a summary of how the gospel has been transmitted by the will of God from Christ—through Paul, through Lois, through Eunice, through Onesiphorus, through many witnesses—to Timothy. Now it is up to Timothy to carry on the line of transmission. He is to depend on "the grace that is in Christ Jesus" (2:1) so that what he has received will be delivered to others, and they in turn will deliver it to those who come after them.

In order to take his place in this line of succession, Timothy must join with those who have preceded him in suffering for the sake of the gospel. Paul uses three metaphors—from military life, athletics, and agriculture—to drive this point home. The metaphors suggest that the "good soldier of Christ Jesus" 2:3) is always a suffering servant. Timothy will learn this lesson, not from human examples, but from his union with the Lord, whose death has "brought life and immortality to light through the gospel" (1:10).

■ **2 Timothy 2:8-13.** Therefore, the "good soldier of Christ Jesus" is sustained in suffering service by remembering Jesus Christ and his victory. Suffering in the preaching of this victory can be endured, even as Paul demonstrates, because the suffering is in the service of the good news that cannot be hindered by imprisonment or silenced by death. Paul's ministry parallels the ministry of Jesus, and is necessary so that God's saving purpose will be realized in those who hear the gospel and are baptized into the household of faith.

In baptism, the baptized person takes part by faith in the death and resurrection of Jesus Christ, but not fully and finally. Christian existence is always a matter of persevering in the faith, dying and rising daily with Christ. Without endurance in suffering, there is no victory. Clergy who deny Christ will themselves be denied by Christ.

This ominous pattern of threatening judgment is broken by the memory that inspired it. Jesus Christ's death and resurrection break the chain of human denial and divine retribution by reversing the assumptions of a religion based on exact retribution. Since God's ways revealed in Christ Jesus are not human ways, when humans are faithless, God remains faithful. The last word for clergy and laity alike is not the defeat of human denial but the absolute victory of God in Christ. Sins are forgiven without condition.

■ **2 Timothy 2:14-19.** Ordained ministers are especially open to the temptations of idle speculation in order to make the gospel more compatible to the standards of the world. Here the ministers are reminded of their responsibility before God to handle the "word of truth" (2:15) rightly by guarding it, preaching it, following it, and suffering for it. To do otherwise is to lead those under their charge into error and destruction, which, like gangrene, will corrupt the whole body.

Two persons, Hymenaeus and Philetus, are mentioned as examples of those "who have departed from the truth" because they say "that the resurrection has already taken place" (2:18). This doctrine is particularly dangerous, for it encourages persons to believe that their salvation is complete and that they have no need to struggle against or to endure suffering from the enemies of God in human history. Such heresy deprives the suffering of Christians of its meaning and is a blasphemy against the cross of Jesus Christ. Christian ministers are delivered from such false teachings, not by what they know is always uncertain, but by the certainty that they are known by God. The realization that their life and teaching is always known to God prompts them to "turn away from wickedness" (2:19) by holding fast to the "word of truth."

■ **2 Timothy 2:20-26.** The household of God is not perfect, but includes men and women who struggle against, and sometimes succumb to, evil. Paul focuses on the responsibility of ordained ministers to consecrate themselves to the service of the truth by aiming at "righteousness, faith, love and peace" (2:22) and by shunning "foolish and stupid arguments" (2:23). Their vocation is to build up the church in unity and harmony by teaching what is patient and kind to those who fall into error. The purpose of teaching the truth is not to win arguments but to win souls. That can be done by relying completely on God to call persons to repent of their errors and accept the truth. Only the loving servant of the Lord is used by God to deliver persons from the satanic bondage of false teaching.

■ **2 Timothy 3:1-9.** The household of faith is a battleground between "lovers of pleasure" and "lovers of God" (3:4). The time of stress in the church is no accident. Just as Christ was opposed by those "having a form of godliness but denying its power" (3:5), so faithful ministers of the gospel suffer at the hands of those who claim to know and do God's will. Such persons are to be avoided because they oppose the truth, the revelation of God's self-giving love in Christ Jesus. The truth of God will prevail. Their folly will be brought to light, and like Jannes and Jambres (thought to be the "wise men" of Exodus 7:11), the opponents of Moses, "they will not get very far" (3:9). The entire passage urges ordained ministers to hold fast to the gospel as the only power that will enable them to endure suffering and resist evil.

■ **2 Timothy 3:10-17.** Paul is the model that Timothy and all the clergy are to follow. He is not the model in terms of his human success. Rather, Paul is the model of how the Lord rescued him from persecutions and suffering by enabling him to endure in faith, patience, love, and endurance. The gospel offers no easy way out, but a way through persecution to a godly life in Christ Jesus. Timothy and the whole body of clergy are delivered from deception by the truth they have received from Paul and other faithful witnesses. What they have received is confirmed by the witness of Scripture—the Hebrew writings and the documents of the early Christian church. These Scriptures witness to God's self-revelation in human history, which equips ordained ministers for their work and sustains them in the persecutions that come to all who follow Christ.

■ **2 Timothy 4:1-5.** Timothy's ministry is not subject to the changing standards of society but to the revelation of God's self-giving love in Christ Jesus. Therefore, his ministry, like the ministry of all clergy, is under the supervision of God and Christ, and is accountable only to them in their redeeming and judging action.

Preaching and teaching are gospel actions. Therefore, they are not occasions for pride, arrogance, or conceit but for unfailing patience. Ordained ministers are called to endure the suffering that faithfulness to the gospel entails by steadfast trust in the gospel to overcome false teaching ("myths," 4:4) and to lead those who wander away from the truth back to sound doctrine. Ministry is fulfilled as it is begun, by following Christ Jesus in the way of the cross.

■ **2 Timothy 4:6-8.** Paul once more refers to his Christian experience as a model for Timothy and other clergy to follow. Paul can no longer do the work of ministry because of his imprisonment and imminent death. So he entrusts the work of ministry to others in the confidence that he has been steadfast in the cause, has persevered until the end, and has not faltered in his allegiance. No matter how his life may seem to be swallowed up in suffering and overwhelmed by death, he lives in hope that the Lord whom he has served by faith will raise him up to eternal life on the day of the Lord's appearing. What Paul claims by faith for himself, he claims by faith for all who live in longing for God's purpose to be fulfilled.

■ **2 Timothy 4:9-18.** Paul's exalted confession of faith that the Lord will complete the work of salvation by giving him eternal life "on that day" (4:8) is not a fanciful flight from the realities of his present situation. Rather, the confession confirms his fellowship with those who have remained loyal to him: Timothy whom he expects to come to him soon, Crescens and Titus who have left him to minister in other places, Luke who alone is with him, Mark whom he expects to come with Timothy, and Tychicus whom he has sent to Ephesus. Paul also has unpleasant memories of those who have failed to meet the test of his suffering and persecution: Demas who has deserted him because of his love for "this world" (4:10), Alexander the metalworker who has done him "a great deal of harm" (4:14), and all who failed to take his part when he was imprisoned. In his desperate need, Paul transcends his concern for his welfare to offer a prayer for those who deserted him: "May it not be held against them" (4:16). This generosity of spirit is possible because Paul remembers that the Lord has not forsaken him and has used his imprisonment as the occasion for his mission to the Gentiles. So in the very jaws of death Paul is confident that the Lord will give him ultimate victory and bring him safely to the heavenly kingdom.

■ **2 Timothy 4:19-22.** In his closing, Paul once again reveals the generosity of his spirit. His thoughts turn to the ties of Christian love that bind him and his co-workers into a community of mutual support. The church is not an idea but a historical witness to God's self-giving love in Christ. That love manifests in the exchange of greetings, in a reminder of the needs of others, and in the longing of an old man to see his young friend.

DIMENSION THREE: WHAT DOES THE BIBLE MEAN TO ME?

2 Timothy 2:24-25—The Need for Kindness and Forbearance in Resisting Evil

Paul mentions several persons who have either deserted him or "departed from the truth" (2:18). However, he never attacks them personally; he simply refers to what they have done. Is this distinction between the evil deed and the person relevant for us in our struggle to overcome evil? Are you able to be kind to those whom you consider a threat to the unity and integrity of the church? How is failure to be "kind to everyone" (2:24) a denial of Christ? What is the connection between being "kind to everyone" and the cross of Jesus Christ?

Paul also urges "the Lord's servant" (2:24) to be forbearing in resisting evildoers. This strategy is not passive but an active taking on of the error of another. Have you ever received this response from some person whom you have wronged? How did it feel? Would you recommend this pattern of resisting evil for the church? Is this the way of the cross?

2 Timothy 3:1-5—The Distinction Between the Form of Religion and the Power of Religion

In Paul's understanding, the power of religion and of the cross is the transforming love of God revealed in Christ Jesus. Is the power of the cross denied in the church today? What are some evidences of denial of the power of the cross? Has the use of the cross as a religious symbol emptied it of its power and made it into a form of religion that denies the power of religion? How can we begin to recover the cross as a means of experiencing anew the self-giving love of God?

For the grace of God has appeared that offers salvation to all people. (2:11)

12

THE LIFE OF GRACE IN THE CHURCH

Titus

DIMENSION ONE: WHAT DOES THE BIBLE SAY?

Answer these questions by reading Titus 1

1. What is Paul's responsibility as "a servant of God and an apostle of Jesus Christ"? (1:1)

2. To whom is the letter sent? (1:4)

3. Where has Titus been left by Paul? Why? (1:5)

4. What group is especially troublesome in Crete? (1:10)

5. How are the Cretans described? (1:12)

Answer these questions by reading Titus 2

6. What is Titus urged to teach? (2:1)

7. Of what is Titus to be an example? (2:7)

8. To whom are slaves to be subject? (2:9)

9. What has appeared for the salvation of all? (2:11)

10. Who gave himself for us to redeem us? (2:13-14)

Answer these questions by reading Titus 3

11. To whom are the Cretans to be subject? (3:1)

12. Why are Christians saved? (3:5)

13. To what are believers in God to devote themselves? (3:8)

14. How many times is a divisive person to be warned? (3:10)

15. Whom does Paul ask Titus to help on their way? (3:13)

DIMENSION TWO: WHAT DOES THE BIBLE MEAN?

■ **Titus 1:14.** Paul writes to Titus in order to address matters of doctrine, conduct, and organization that threaten the life of the early church. The purpose of the letter is to resolve these matters by appealing to Paul's authoritative gospel as it was given and preserved in the church.

The little that we know about Titus has been summarized by one scholar as follows:

> Titus, a Gentile Christian, concerning whom Acts, strange to say, is silent, is first named by Paul in Gal. 2:1, 3, as one of his companions on the journey to the apostolic council, where the Apostle successfully withstood the demand to circumcise Titus. According to II Corinthians, he delivered the "intermediate epistle" to the Corinthian congregation. He settled the discord which existed between Paul and Corinth, and actively promoted the business of the collection (2:13; 7:6f., 13ff.), and after the fulfillment of this mission he once more came from Macedonia with II Corinthians as forerunner of Paul to Corinth (8:6, 16ff.; 12:18). II Tim. 4:10 speaks yet of a journey of Titus from Rome, where he was with Paul, to Dalmatia.[1]

Paul and Titus were bound together in the household of God by their common faith. Faith here has a definite content: faith is the fulfillment of God's saving purpose in Jesus Christ. Knowledge of this truth is given to God's chosen people through Paul's preaching of the gospel. The result of his preaching is godly behavior sustained by hope

1 Werner Georg Kümmel, *Introduction to the New Testament* 17th rev. ed., trans. Howard Clark Kee (Nashville: Abingdon Press, 1975), 370.

of eternal life. Paul's ministry of the word is authoritative because it is "by the command of God our Savior" (1:3). "Grace and peace" (1:4) summarize the action of God in the gospel and the results of that action in the church. Paul is the agent of grace and peace in the church, but the ultimate source is "God the Father and Christ Jesus our Savior" (1:4).

■ **Titus 1:5-8.** The church does not automatically live in grace and peace. If the line of faithful transmission of the gospel from Paul to Titus to the clergy under his supervision is broken, dependence on God's love revealed in Christ may be replaced by false teaching, and the peace of the community may be destroyed by quarrels and divisions. To avoid this danger, Paul left Titus on Crete to appoint elders as overseers or bishops in every town.

The requirements for serving as a presiding elder are ethical because the acid test of sound doctrine is right living. Elders meet this test by showing in their private lives that their relationships to their wives and children are ordered by the gospel. Also, as God's stewards in the public realm, they are required to live for others by restraining every selfish impulse and by cultivating attitudes and actions that build up the community of faith.

■ **Titus 1:9-16.** The basic function of presiding elders, as understood by Paul, is transmission of the "trustworthy message" or "sound doctrine" (1:9). Clergy are empowered for right conduct in the private and public spheres by holding firm to the gospel they received from Paul. That same gospel enables them to contradict the heresies of false teachers. The intensity of Paul's attack on the false teachers indicates that they are present in Crete in large numbers and attracting many followers.

The false teachers seem to be Gentile Christians who insist that the church is still under the Jewish ritual laws. These false teachers are denounced as greedy charlatans and liars, who have rejected the revealed truth for myths based on human speculation. They are to be silenced and rebuked in the hope that they may repent. They are especially dangerous because they hold that evil is in certain created things instead of admitting that evil arises from their corrupted minds and consciences. Their false teaching is revealed in their deeds. Since they trust their misguided knowledge, they deny God by "detestable, disobedient" (1:16) behavior.

■ **Titus 2:1-10.** The role of Titus in straightening out "what was left unfinished" (1:5) in Crete is to "teach what is appropriate to sound doctrine" (2:1). Here the practical concern of the letter is paramount. "What is appropriate to sound doctrine" is obedience to the gospel in whatever age group or social class the Christian finds himself or herself. The specific instructions laid down in these verses for older men, older women, younger women, younger men, and slaves are not uniquely Christian; they are paralleled in the moral standards of the ancient world. What is distinctive about them here is the insistence that they are the actions that accompany sound doctrine, that failure to obey them will discredit the gospel in the pagan world, and that all Christians must live according to the gospel. No suggestion is given that clergy must meet higher standards than the laity or that bishops are more accountable than slaves.

The unifying theme running through the whole section is that hearing the gospel of God's self-giving love results in living the gospel of God's self-giving love in all conditions and in all relationships. In verses 7 and 8, Paul urges Titus to embody in his deeds and express in his speech the good news of Jesus Christ.

■ **Titus 2:11-15.** The source of Christian conduct is the life and ministry of Jesus that has been given by God for the salvation of all. "The grace of God" (2:11) is not an abstract idea but the self-disclosure of God in the life, death, and resurrection of Jesus. That grace continues to be present in the church in the preaching of the gospel that enables the faithful to turn from idolatry and self-indulgence to dependence on God and self-giving service. The life of the church is always a life of hope, because the faithful await the completion of God's saving work, "the appearing of the glory of our great God and Savior, Jesus Christ" (2:13). Until that day of victory over sin and death—through the resurrection of the dead—the church witnesses to its faith by living "self-controlled, upright and godly lives in this present age" (2:12).

All that Paul has urged Titus to teach the men, the women, and the slaves is possible because the self-giving love of Jesus frees all persons from self-centeredness and sets them apart as people consecrated to God's work in the world. They obey God, not as a burdensome duty, but as the grateful response of a purified and redeemed people. Titus has received this message, and is now authorized to guard and transmit it. His message is authoritative because it is revealed by God in Jesus. It has power because it is the grace of God at work in his life. It commands respect because it points beyond itself to "the appearing of the glory of our great God and Savior, Jesus Christ."

■ **Titus 3:1-8a.** Up to this point the letter has focused on the organization of the church, transmission of sound doctrine, and the duties of Christians to one another. Now, quite abruptly, the center of attention shifts to a consideration of the responsibilities of Christians in a non-Christian world. Titus is urged to emphasize obedience to rulers and authorities, not as a grudging necessity, but as a willing participation in work for the common good. This devotion to civil service requires not only respect for public officials but also courtesy, gentleness, and respect for all persons. Christians are required to live at peace in the world as well as in the church, and to do so by refusing to take part in quarrels and by abstaining from slanderous speech.

All this is simply extending the requirement to love the brothers and sisters in the church to include love for all persons. Including outsiders is not motivated by a desire to please the world but by memory of God's absolutely inclusive love in Jesus Christ. Since all the brothers and sisters in the church were included by God's kindness and love while they were foolish, disobedient sinners, they are obligated to show perfect courtesy to all persons.

The household of God is not just another social institution. It is the work of God in Jesus Christ. God's household is always in the world but not of the world, for the church is created by God's grace on behalf of those without merit. The dramatic enactment of the gospel in baptism is empowered by the Holy Spirit, so that the church is the community of those who look by faith for the gift of eternal life. To live in hope is to show forth the power of God's grace by doing honest work in the public sphere and being gentle and courteous to all people. We may speculate about some things, but about this there is no question: "This is a trustworthy saying" (3:8a).

■ **Titus 3:8b-11.** Sound doctrine and good deeds are inseparable. Those who receive the truth and obey it will be distinguished by the quality of their lives. Conversely, those who are attracted by "foolish controversies and genealogies and arguments and quarrels about the law" (3:9) will have no interest in good deeds. Rather, they will pursue their interests at the expense of the welfare of the church and the general public. Since the teachers of false doctrine and their followers pose an immediate threat to the life and work of the church, they are to be excluded from the community. The discipline of the church is simply the public confirmation of their self-condemnation.

■ **Titus 3:12-15.** As Paul concludes this letter to Titus, he applies the content of the letter to their relationship. He gives himself to Titus by offering to send Artemas or Tychicus to Crete. He urges Titus to do his best to come to him and to send Zenas and Apollos on their way with adequate provisions for their needs. This mutual concern is the conduct of a people who "devote themselves to doing what is good" (3:14). Titus and Paul are teachers of sound doctrine, as they demonstrate in their personal behavior what it means to help cases of urgent need by being fruitful in love. The grace of God binds them together in spite of their physical separation, and enables them to experience a community of faith and love, redeemed and purified by Jesus Christ. Sending and receiving greetings is not a mere formality. Rather, it is a sign that God's salvation has appeared in the world.

DIMENSION THREE: WHAT DOES THE BIBLE MEAN TO ME?

Titus 2:1-14—Relationships Among Christians in the Church

Regardless of age, sex, or status, the gospel redeems persons from selfish living and purifies them for self-giving service. Does this apply to clergy and laity alike? Have you experienced zeal for "doing what is good" (2:6) in your local church? What examples can you recall of Christians giving themselves for one another in worship, in teaching, in service projects?

One strength of Paul's instructions to Titus is his willingness to deal with specific relationships. How can we apply his teaching about the responsibilities of older men, younger men, older women, younger women, and slaves to our lives? Have you noticed that Paul seems to disregard the subject of rights while focusing on the subject of responsibilities? Is this emphasis needed in the modern church? List specific responsibilities we have as Christians to our spouses, our children, our friends, our leaders, and to the vulnerable among us. Relate these responsibilities to the grace of God.

Titus 3:1-8—Relationships Between Christians and the World

God's love redeemed us, not because of our goodness, but by virtue of grace alone. Therefore, as Christians, we are to manifest in our relationships to the world the love God has shown us in Jesus Christ our Savior. How does this apply to our participation in government? Is it relevant for our attitude toward our public officials and civil servants? Does it require us to be active in community affairs?

Christians cannot restrict their love to members of the church but must "always be gentle toward everyone" (3:2). Does this mean that Christians in public life should be more concerned with responsibilities than with rights? Do you emphasize an inclusive morality in your local church? How is civic responsibility related to the work of the Holy Spirit? Can you make a connection between the ritual of baptism and the obligation to be a good citizen?

I do wish, brother, that I may have some benefit from you in the Lord; refresh my heart in Christ. (20)

13

CHRISTIAN REFRESHMENT

Philemon

DIMENSION ONE: WHAT DOES THE BIBLE SAY?

Answer these questions by reading Philemon

1. To whom is the letter written? (1)

2. Who else is included in the salutation? (2)

3. Why does Paul thank God always? (4-5)

4. What has Paul derived from Philemon's love? (7)

5. How does Paul identify himself? (9)

6. Whose father does Paul become in his imprisonment? (10)

7. Whom does Paul send back to Philemon? (10, 12)

8. Does Paul want Philemon's goodness to be spontaneous or forced? (14)

9. How is Philemon to receive Onesimus? (15-16)

10. Who will repay what Onesimus owes Philemon? (18-19)

11. Of what is Paul confident? (21)

12. What does Paul ask Philemon to prepare for him? (22)

13. Who is Paul's fellow prisoner? (23)

14. Who are Paul's fellow workers? (24)

DIMENSION TWO: WHAT DOES THE BIBLE MEAN?

■ **Philemon 1-3.** Once again, Paul is writing from prison. Quite likely the letter's destination is Colossae, for Onesimus and Archippus are both located there, according to Colossians 4:9. The letter is intensely personal in that it contains Paul's direct appeal to a wealthy Christian, Philemon, to welcome back his runaway slave, Onesimus, as a brother. But the letter is also intentionally corporate, for the relationship between Philemon and Onesimus is a matter that involves the Christian community at Colossae and throughout the world.

Paul and Philemon share a common task; they are fellow workers. As a "dear friend and fellow worker" (v. 1), Philemon's welfare is of supreme importance to Paul. The letter focuses on Philemon's response to the return of Onesimus and is written so that Philemon will remember who he is, and will act accordingly. Although the letter may seem to be concerned with the fate of Onesimus, it actually concentrates exclusively on the decision Philemon must make.

Paul counts on the Christian community at Colossae to support Philemon in making his decision about Onesimus. Apphia is probably Philemon's literal sister, but she is also Paul's sister in the church. The church is understood figuratively as a family, and the family ties are the nurturing relationships that bind the members together and control their actions. But the church is not only a family. It is also an army under orders. Paul, Apphia, Archippus, Philemon, and all the saints are fellow soldiers. They are a disciplined community, subject at all times to the commands of a higher authority. If the members of the community disobey those orders, their life as brothers and sisters and fellow workers is in great jeopardy.

Thus, Philemon's response to the crisis of the return of Onesimus involves the whole Christian community, even as it finds concrete expression in the church that meets in his house. What Paul expects Philemon to do is made known at Rome and at Colossae, so that the issue is no longer a matter that involves a master and his slave but a decision that will either build up the household of God or threaten its existence as a disciplined community of brothers and sisters.

The household of God is a concrete and specific community, located in a particular place and at a definite time. The community is made up of real people in their relationships to one another as they struggle with personal and social problems. Yet it is always a community that transcends its time and place because of its origin in God and its obedience to Jesus Christ. The church at Colossae in Philemon's house is the creation of God's grace. *Grace*, in this context, refers to the powerful action of God in Jesus Christ that calls the community into existence and sustains it in obedience. The result of God's action in Christ is the peace or total well-being of the community that the brothers and sisters enjoy now by faith and will experience fully at the coming of Christ.

The church receives its unique character and distinctive mission, not from its historical or social or cultural context, but from its relationship to God revealed in Jesus Christ. It is at Colossae, but it is of God. The church meets in Philemon's house under Philemon's leadership, but it takes orders from Jesus Christ alone. Therefore, the only relationships that have absolute relevance for the faith and action of the church are, not the literal relationships of its history, society, and culture, but the figurative relationships of its faith summarized in the apostolic benediction: "Grace to you and peace from God our Father and the Lord Jesus Christ" (v. 3). Since the source of the community is the power of God revealed in Jesus Christ, the ultimate allegiance of the church is expressed in obedience to Jesus Christ as Lord of all. The body of the letter that follows shows how the parenthood of God and the lordship of Jesus Christ mandate what Philemon must do to receive Onesimus in the family of God.

■ **Philemon 4-7.** The reality that unites Paul with Philemon is God. That reality is not an abstraction; God is the One with whom Paul communes in prayer and to whom Paul offers thanks. His thanksgiving is the characteristic attitude of his life that always is inspired by recalling the effect of the gospel in the life of Philemon (v. 4). Paul's gratitude to God is not conditioned by the uncertain circumstances of his life. Rather, it springs from the knowledge that God is at work in his ministry, bringing persons to faith and enabling them to persevere in the face of trials and tribulations.

The work of the gospel in Philemon is love and faith, which is focused primarily on the Lord Jesus, but which also, necessarily, includes "all [God's] holy people" (v. 5). The word *love* is the basis of all that Paul will develop later in the body of the letter. *Love* here means active good will directed toward another, and is the norm for behavior within the household of God. Philemon has a reputation for practicing this love, and Paul prays that he will not falter in extending it to Onesimus. Paul is not concerned simply for the life of the community but also expresses a missionary strategy, which affirms that the sharing of faith through love promotes the spread of the gospel in the world. The world comes to know "every good thing we share for the sake of Christ" (v. 6) as the church obeys the gospel in love for the brothers and sisters.

Paul has been given "joy and encouragement," not by what Philemon has done for him directly, but by what he has done to refresh "the hearts of the saints" (v. 7). The force of the argument depends on Paul's identification of himself as Philemon's "brother" (v. 7) and his enlargement of the family circle through "God our Father and the Lord Jesus Christ" (v. 3) to include all the household of God. Philemon is Paul's brother in the same way that he is the brother of all the saints. If Philemon falters in receiving and refreshing Onesimus as his brother, then he also fails to receive and refresh Paul.

■ **Philemon 8-14.** Paul has no doubt about what the gospel requires of Philemon in relationship to Onesimus. What Philemon "ought to do" (v. 8) is receive and refresh Onesimus as a brother. As an apostle entrusted with the gospel of Christ by God, Paul has authority to command Philemon. But he renounces this approach to the problem as a contradiction of the gospel. Since the gospel is essentially the self-giving love of God, the only way to serve the gospel is through self-giving love, which alone is able to create self-giving love. "On the basis of love" (v. 9) is another way of saying for God's sake or for Christ's sake or for the gospel's sake. Since Paul is an ambassador of God's self-giving love in the world, he is a "prisoner" (v. 9) in the world without authority, except as he depends on the authority of the gospel to do God's work in the world.

The only thing in doubt in Paul's mind is how Philemon will respond to Onesimus. So Paul appeals to Philemon, not on the basis of the master-slave relationship of the world, but on the basis of the complex relationships of life in the household of God. Paul, in the gospel, is Onesimus's "father," and Onesimus in the gospel is Paul's "son" (v. 10). In his imprisonment, in his powerlessness, Paul has been the instrument of the gospel that has converted Onesimus from a useless slave to a useful member of the household of God.

Conversion, however, has not taken Onesimus out of the world. Rather, it has called him to live in the world as a child of God and a slave of the Lord Jesus Christ. Therefore, Paul sends him back to his master so that he and his master may witness to the new relationship that is theirs in Jesus Christ. Paul has already entered into that relationship, as Onesimus has become a part of his life and ministry in his imprisonment. Now Paul wants Philemon to have that same experience; but it cannot be coerced. Life in the household of God is always life under the freedom of God's love that awaits the decision of faith in the concrete circumstances of life. Everything hangs in the balance. Paul is sending Philemon's slave back to him so that Philemon can consent to receive him as a brother in Christ "and not [be] forced" (v. 14).

■ **Philemon 15-20.** Paul knows of no realm of human experience devoid of God's action. Therefore, he sees Onesimus's running away as providential, in the sense that it is the occasion for the experience of the gospel's transforming power in the world. The master-slave relationship of the flesh is destined to come to an end, but the relationship of brothers in the Lord is forever. Onesimus is now infinitely more precious than a piece of property.

He is "a dear brother" (v. 16) to not only Paul but also Philemon. Philemon is challenged to welcome Onesimus as "a dear brother" in the world and in the church, "both as a fellow man and as a brother in the Lord" (v. 16).

How Philemon responds will determine his relationship to not only Onesimus but also Paul. If Philemon desires to continue as Paul's "partner" (v. 17) in evangelism, then he must receive Onesimus as he would receive Paul. Partnership in the gospel is not a status but a function that exists only in conformity to the gospel. The issue is drawn clearly. If Philemon excludes Onesimus from the church in his house, the church will meet elsewhere, Philemon will forfeit his ministry, and he himself will be excluded.

Paul's identification with Onesimus is real. He assumes all Onesimus's debts and obligations, and converts the offer to pay into a legal document by taking pen in hand and signing his name. This action opens up a final argument, as it reminds Paul that Philemon stands in the same relationship to Paul as Onesimus. In the gospel, he is their father and they are his children. Just as Onesimus owes Paul his life in the gospel, so Philemon owes him his life in the gospel. Philemon can repay Paul by giving him "some benefit" (v. 20), by living under the lordship of Christ, by receiving Onesimus as "a dear brother." The only way Philemon can "refresh" (v. 20) Paul's heart is by offering the hospitality of his house to Onesimus.

■ **Philemon 21-22.** Since Paul has based his appeal to Philemon on the authority of God's self-giving love in Christ, he is confident that the ministry of that love will evoke the response of faith in Philemon. He knows that the gospel has power to convince and compel in ways that transcend Paul's expectations and exhortations. So Paul leaves the outcome of the matter open, knowing that Philemon "will do even more than" (v. 21) he says. This confidence in the gospel also reassures Paul about his relationship to Philemon. His letter will prevail. Philemon will welcome Onesimus as "a dear brother." If Paul is released from prison through Philemon's prayers, he will look forward to occupying a guest room in his house; for it is God's house, where all are brothers and sisters under the master of the house, the Lord Jesus Christ.

■ **Philemon 23-25.** The concluding greetings serve to remind Philemon and the church in his house that they belong to a worldwide community that cannot be broken or impeded by imprisonment. Sharing in the gospel is not simply a local experience but also universal, because it is life under the parenthood of God and the lordship of Jesus Christ. Paul and Philemon and Mark and Aristarchus and Demas and Luke minister in different ways in different places. However, they are united in the ministry that arises from God's love in Christ, shares that love, and promotes it in the world. Since the grace of the Lord Jesus Christ is with Philemon's spirit, he is empowered to receive all as beloved members of the household of God "as a fellow man and as a brother in the Lord" (v. 16), in the world and in the church.

DIMENSION THREE: WHAT DOES THE BIBLE MEAN TO ME?

Philemon 4-7—The Scope of Christian Refreshment

All Christians need refreshment or rest from work that restores and renews strength. None is self-sufficient, and all require the ministry of the community in order to persevere as faithful witnesses to the gospel. Do you acknowledge this need in your life? Are you sensitive to the need of persons in leadership roles for the refreshment of community support? Do you feel that adequate attention to the need for refreshment is given in your church?

Refreshment in this context is a matter of the "heart," the essential core of human existence. To refresh the heart is to restore and renew the strength of the whole person. How are your needs for physical, emotional, intellectual, and spiritual refreshment being met by your church community? Is this a self-conscious concern of the church that is given high priority and careful attention? How is Christian refreshment an essential component of evangelism?

Philemon 15-20—The Source of Christian Refreshment

Refreshment is not withdrawal from the world but being in the world as a community of grace and peace, a community of obedience to God's action in Jesus Christ. Are you refreshed when you hear reports of the faith and love of the church? What specific instances of this refreshment can you recall?

The attitude and action of receiving Onesimus as a beloved brother were sure to create controversy in Colossae, but Paul urged Philemon to obey the gospel. He beseeched him to "refresh my heart in Christ" (v. 20). How can we be refreshed by the Christian community if we simply settle for the attitudes and actions that are accepted by our culture? Does Christian refreshment always involve conflict with the forces of inequality and injustice? If we are not refreshed by the Christian community, is that a sign that the community itself has lost its sense of calling and mission?

About the Writer

Dr. Van Bogard Dunn was Professor Emeritus and Dean Emeritus at the Methodist Theological School in Ohio, Delaware, Ohio.